"Tradition starts as heresy."

David Grisman, p. 133

Contents

ON THE COVER

There's Americana music and folk, alt-country and blues, Ameripolitan, cowpunk, country, and rock. There are so many words we can use to describe this music that speaks to so many of us. But underneath it all are deep roots that were planted way back when all of it was just called music. Those are the roots that are tapped whenever we gather in a room or a field, at a jam or a festival. The roots of this music connect us not only to one another, but to the long line of musicians and songwriters who have handed down the music from fiddle to guitar, from mouth to ear, for generations. So it seemed time for us to dedicate an issue to some of these roots and the branches they've produced. When we handed the task of designing our cover to Waco Brothers frontman and accomplished painter Jon Langford, he delivered a pair of trees that are completely different at first glance. But when you back away, you realize their roots are intimately entwined.

Inside covers
Two Lyrics from One Song
Illustrations by Drew Christie.

NO DEPRESSION TEAM
Chris Wadsworth *Publisher*
Kim Ruehl *Editor*
Stacy Chandler *Copy Editor/Social Media Manager*
Dave Champine *Problem Solver*
Shelley Champine *QA/Community Manager*
Sonja Nelson *Advertising*

WEB nodepression.com
TWITTER & INSTAGRAM @nodepression
FACEBOOK facebook.com/nodepression

GENERAL INQUIRIES
info@nodepression.com

ADVERTISING
advertising@nodepression.com

MAGAZINE DESIGN & PRODUCTION
Brett Yasko, with thanks to *Fretboard Journal*
Printed in Canada by Hemlock Printers

No Depression is part of the FreshGrass Foundation.
freshgrass.com
ISBN: 978-0-9973317-1-4
©2016, FreshGrass, LLC

Hello Stranger

BY KIM RUEHL

There's an old African proverb: "Without roots, a tree cannot stand."

And while we throw around the phrase "roots music" with wild abandon these days – I've been known to explain to strangers at parties that it's "anything with a banjo or fiddle," knowing full well that does not suffice – the magnetic pull of cultural relevance, article clicks, and a need to build an audience keeps us all too often chattering about the branches.

No doubt, what's happening at the end of a branch – whether it's John Fullbright or Nikki Lane, Ruby Amanfu or Front Country – is exciting. Youth and vitality tug at the eye. Catchy choruses and surprising licks entice the ear. These artists are *now*, after all, and their ability to be so of this moment in history helps contextualize us, the listeners. We feel a part of something when they open their mouths. But when we pause to home in on what's happening with the music, we realize that the bits getting under our skin, pushing up the goosebumps – those are echoes of Woody and Pete, of Hank and Loretta, of Sister Rosetta and David Grisman. We realize that, on some almost cellular level, the music finds something unconscious in us, something we've never explored, something that was handed down.

When we pause to step away from the fleeting emotion and peer into the song, we notice that branch is connected to something.

As I write this, the small woods behind my house are blanketed in more than a foot of snow. It's natural to look up at times like these, to marvel at how lines of snow can stretch all the way to the tip of those long branches, which grow thinner as they reach away from the trunk. But even in this thick, wintry, beautiful dormancy, I can choose to remember the roots underground. The way they always grip the earth, no matter what weather is passing above, holding not only the ground together but the branches aloft.

It's with this image in mind that I consider the music. It makes the notion of "roots music" light up and dance. Suddenly, this music we love is not a trend or a social circle or even a community. It's a life force. It's past, present, and future. It's foundation and growth, digging deeper even as it stretches outward. It's balance, and like the tree whose metaphor I just can't let go, it exists to help us breathe without thinking. It's there for all of us.

It makes sense, then, that we here at *No Depression* have shifted our quasi-autonomous operations in order to exist alongside the FreshGrass Festival, under the FreshGrass Foundation, a nonprofit fund founded by our publisher, Chris Wadsworth. With the Foundation, we can turn around the money we make from this journal and provide financial gifts to artists and communities, commission

long musical works, and sponsor music-making opportunities in towns and cities across the country. While there's infinite value in simply telling stories, we felt we needed to answer the question "Where does the money go?" And no sooner did we ask it than the answer became clear: it goes back to the roots.

So, get comfortable and settle into these stories – stories about the way this music has branched out over centuries, stood for the people, actively resisted oppression, shined light in darkness, transcended loneliness, and borne infinite fruit. Some of these stories are unexpected, like the sweeping influence of an 18th-century Scottish poet; others, like that of Sister Rosetta Tharpe, have been all but forgotten. Still others – the rise of Oklahoma, the twists and turns of the harmonica – are widely known and little understood. It's my hope that these stories may help you remember not only how ever-present our roots are, but also how vital their health is to the ways in which we grow.

NO DEPRESSION

THE PLOUGH-MAN POET

How Robert Burns laid the foundation for the American folk revival

by Scott Alarik

A Poet's Welcome

C v = fo 279

Thou's welcome ...
If thoughts o' thee
Shall ever daunte...

Or if I blush

Tho' now they
And tease my name
The maid they talk

An auld wife's tongue

Welcome, my bon...
Tho' ye come
And tho' yous

Yet by my faith

Sweet fruit
My funny

MARC HARKNESS

> **"You skipped the big town street just like I done,
> you ducked the crosstown cops just like I ducked.
> Your talking was factual figures of the biggest sort.
> Your talking had the graphboard and the chart
> and had something else most singers seem to
> miss, the very kiss of warm dew on the stalk."**
>
> *To That Man Robert Burns*
> by Woody Guthrie, 1947

WHEN BOB DYLAN WAS ASKED, as part of record chain HMV's *My Inspiration* campaign, to name his greatest creative inspiration, he did not name Woody Guthrie, as many would have guessed. Instead, he picked Robert Burns, whom Guthrie believed he was related to, and cited the 18th-century Scottish poet as both a political and songwriting hero.

Burns' influence on America goes much deeper than his influence on two of our greatest songwriters. For his first published song, "Old Dog Tray," Stephen Foster borrowed a melody from a Burns song. Ralph Waldo Emerson wrote that the Declaration of Independence and the Rights of Man "are no more weighty documents in the history of freedom than are the songs of Robert Burns."

It is nearly impossible to find an American literary giant who did not claim Burns as an essential influence. Thomas Jefferson actually cited him as the supreme proof that an American vernacular literature would elevate our culture. Washington Irving's Hudson River home was covered in Scottish ivy brought to him by a woman for whom Burns had written a love song. Edgar Allen Poe, Henry Wadsworth Longfellow, Walt Whitman, John Greenleaf Whittier, and Mark Twain all wrote of his importance to them, and to American literature.

A young Abraham Lincoln regaled his New Salem neighbors by reciting Burns' epic poem "Tam O'Shanter" in dialect and character voices. Burns' lovely ode to women, "Green Grow the Rashes," was so commonly sung by American soldiers in the Mexican War that the first two words of the chorus (green grow) are believed to be the source of the Mexican idiom "gringo." When abolitionist Frederick Douglass escaped slavery, the first book he purchased with wages he'd earned as a free man was a volume of Burns. Two of the greatest American novels of the 20th century – John Steinbeck's *Of Mice and Men* and J.D. Salinger's *Catcher in the Rye* – were named for lines in Burns' writing.

And yet Robert Burns was born in 1759, before any such place as the United States existed, thousands of miles away in Ayer, Scotland, the son of a poor tenant farmer. Today, he is seen by most Americans in the context of those faraway places and long-ago times, rather than in the light of the early American parlors, libraries, and music halls where his writing was so important to the creation of a distinctly American music and literature.

To be sure, Burns' best songs were as much a part of the foundational American folk canon as any traditional music carried here in immigrant boats. Nearly all 19th-century Americans knew "Comin' Through the Rye," "My Love Is Like a Red, Red Rose," "Ae Fond Kiss," "Flow Gently, Sweet Afton," "Green Grow the Rashes," his populist anthem "A Man's a Man For a' That," and of course, "Auld Lang Syne."

"When you're listening to Stephen Foster, or anyone who came after, you're still, in a way, listening to Robert Burns," says American singer-songwriter Diana Jones. A winner of the Kerrville New Folk songwriting competition who was named Emerging Artist of the Year by the North American Folk Alliance in 2006, Jones has long studied and admired Burns' songwriting.

"What I see is this trail that leads back, like skipping a stone across a pond, from today's songwriters back to Johnny Cash and then to Woody Guthrie and the Carter Family, then that long line back to Stephen Foster. And yet, when you take that legacy and lineage all the way back, it seems to begin with Burns.

"He broke open a whole new way of thinking about what you could write about," she adds, "and that you were okay writing from where you were, as opposed to writing for the upper classes on their terms. Burns showed it was okay to be who you were, and create art from your whole life. You know, they call Johnny Cash the people's writer, who wrote for the dispossessed. And that's really what Burns did, writing in people's vernacular, songs about love and work and death, the things the traditional songs were about."

Because of Burns' genius for writing verse in the language of ordinary people, in an age when nearly all writers sought to write in an erudite, formal style, Burns created phrases that entered our everyday language. We quote Burns every day without realizing it: "do or die," "a silk purse from a sow's ear," "man's inhumanity to man," "the best laid schemes of mice and men," "to see ourselves as others see us," and even "clean as a whistle" were all culled from Burns.

Eric Peltoniemi, who writes populist musicals and naturalistic songs and is the president of respected folk indie label Red House Records, hears the best of today's folk songwriters and recognizes Burns' influence on those who influenced today's music. "Burns was doing what folk people much later tried to do," he explains, "taking traditional melodies and putting his own words to them. And he had this political angle, using his songs to speak up for the common people. He also did a lot to collect and preserve the heritage of folk music. That's exactly what Woody Guthrie and Pete Seeger were doing. Burns was the original professional songwriter, in terms of what people are doing today."

Like so many American roots musicians today, Scotland's Karine Polwart is equally at home with fiddle tunes or folk songs, ancient ballads or her own edgy political anthems. She sees Burns' ability to fuse traditional and modern styles as crucial to his lasting impact.

"He was incredibly musically gifted," she says. "Most of his songs are set to old fiddle and pipe tunes, and his knowledge of that music was vast. He used what was around him and managed to make his ideas find their perfect home. So he was effectively sampling stuff from all around him, not only bits of melody but entire tunes and bits of song that already existed, extending them or pinching little pieces and recasting them. To me, he's got the sensibility of somebody who would be working in the dance [music] scene right now, pecking bits from here and there. He had that foraging mindset."

A Fiddler-Poet, a Scottish Bard

Like his disciple Woody Guthrie, Burns' life was a shooting star, burning impossibly bright and extinguishing too soon. He died at 37, in 1796, probably of a chronic heart disease that was either congenital or contracted during a childhood spent working in his father's fields. Just as Guthrie was later "The Dust Bowl Troubadour," Burns was dubbed "The Ploughman Poet," as an homage to his hardscrabble roots.

Also like Guthrie, Burns' brief artistic life was astonishingly prolific. He wrote nearly 400 songs and collected hundreds more traditional tunes – Burns said that "Auld Lang Syne" was a traditional song he'd collected from an old man. He was also among the most important of the Romantic poets, devoutly studied by William Wordsworth, John Keats, Percy Shelley, Samuel Coleridge, and others.

After rising quickly to literary fame, Burns turned his back on the elite society that had embraced him – even offering him a chance to run for Parliament, the surest route to gentrification for someone so humbly born. But he had other ambitions. In his first book, he dubbed himself "a Scottish Bard, proud of the name, and whose highest ambition is to sing in his Country's service." He did not mean that in the way Britain describes Shakespeare, as its national poet, but in the lineage of the anonymous bards who created traditional music. Burns described himself as a "fiddler-poet," and meant it exactly the way the term "singer-songwriter" is used today: a musician who writes songs. He wanted to be the people's songwriter, not a gentleman poet.

True to form, while in Edinburgh, Burns was talking to a beggar in the streets. A society matron scolded him for being seen in the company of "such a raggedy man." Looking angrily at the woman, Burns replied, "I was talking to the man, mu'um, not the clothes."

In that class-bound age, it's difficult to imagine what that must have meant to the beggar – or to the matron. To Burns, it may have been a cue that he was beginning to live a false life. He soon left Edinburgh, and spent the rest of his

"They call Johnny Cash the people's writer, who wrote for the dispossessed. And that's really what Burns did, writing in people's vernacular, songs about love and work and death."

Diana Jones

life among his own common people, hearing their stories, collecting their folk tunes, playing music with them in cozy country pubs – and writing their songs.

That egalitarian approach to songwriting mattered enormously to a post-Revolutionary America seeking to create a new kind of culture, not defined by its ruling class but by its ordinary citizens. America's is a people's culture, and Burns was a people's songwriter. His great success validated the idea of a distinctly American music and literature, written in the everyday language of ordinary people.

"It's very hard to overestimate what a great influence Burns had on all factors of American life: writers, musicians, educators, and just common people, because his songs and poems were so well known," says Nancy Groce, a folklife specialist at the Library of Congress who has extensively studied Burns' impact on American culture. "The lost art of recitation was taken very seriously in the early 19th century, and Burns, because of his understanding of meter and folk song, had been a pro at writing pieces that could be recited by ordinary people. Add to that his republican sensibility, which echoed the early American pride at breaking free from the monarchy and placing value on the common person."

In an essay titled "America's Bard" for the 2012 scholarly book, *Robert Burns and Transatlantic Culture*, Burns biographer Robert Crawford focused on how important Burns' songs were to those early Americans. "If we think of Burns' language not simply in terms of dialect but of fidelity to – and modification of – vernacular," Crawford writes, "we can see how and why this poet continued to matter to so many American readers … [as well as] politicians and poets across the 19th-century United States."

Beyond that, Burns essentially reversed the energy flow of how professional musicians treated folk music. Before him, the impulse had been to remove traditional music from

its low-born environs and gentrify it. Fiddle tunes were converted into chamber music; the legendary Irish harpist Turlough O'Carolan wrote concertos; madrigals were artfully composed to simulate the earthy passions of folk songs in ways the elite would find inoffensive.

Burns wrote about common people, eye to eye and heart to heart, using their words, their struggles and dreams, their vision and vocabulary. Even more importantly, he wrote *for* them. His goal was to write songs that ordinary people could use in their everyday lives, songs of work and woe, birth and death, mirth and terror, love and loss, war and landscape. There was no natural marketplace for songs like that in Burns' lifetime, though – a detail he finessed by simply refusing to accept money for his songwriting after he left Edinburgh, saying it would feel like "sodomy of the soul" to be paid for creating songs from the commonly owned fields of tradition. In that, he expressed a conflict felt by many folk songwriters who followed him. To support his family while he traveled, he later worked as an excise man, or tax collector.

A few years after his death, however, the Industrial Revolution created the perfect marketplace for the kind of music America was so hungry to consume. Advances in manufacturing led to an explosion in mass-printing of cheap sheet music and songbooks. The same manufacturing advances made it possible to mass-produce inexpensive pianos, once status symbols that only the elite could afford. Americans took great pride in having a piano in their parlor, stacking them with professional songbooks and gathering around while Mother accompanied the nightly sings.

"Burns became part of a larger movement tied into home music-making," says Groce. "This all tied into the rise of the middle class and establishing a commercial music for that middle class.

Burns fit right into that, with his slightly elevated form of folk songs. And the American songwriters who followed him, like Stephen Foster, also aimed for that. But because Burns had such status, singing his songs in the parlor was very popular in early 19th-century America."

The fact that Burns was such a famous and respected poet gave legitimacy to this new kind of professional songwriting, aimed at middle- and working-class consumers. It required a new title to distinguish it from both folk and art music. For a while, it was known as parlor music. When that grew too narrow, it became known as popular music – commercial music for the people.

Burns' songs became staples in the early 19th-century music halls from which so many of America's first popular songwriters emerged, and they were commonly included in "songsters," souvenir books sold by itinerant entertainers. More than any other writer, Burns made it fashionable to create modern songs from folk sources.

The Original Folk Songwriter

While Burns had always written vernacular poems and songs, along with the formal Romantic poetry of the day, his departure from Edinburgh in 1787 marked a radical change toward what would become known as popular songwriting. That change went far beyond his use of folk melodies.

In his wonderful Burns biography, *The Bard*, Crawford writes, "His songwriting changed importantly during this period, becoming less about self-expression than being a spokesman for others – a true folk bard. He wrote songs clearly in other people's voices – their lives, their stories – such as 'My Love Is Like a Red, Red Rose,' and kind-eyed reworkings of a bawdy song, 'John Anderson, My Jo,' turning the lament about an old man's impotence into a tender paean of love."

The first step in this new approach for Burns was an extensive field-collecting journey through Scotland. If he was to be the nation's bard, he needed to learn all its dialects and slang. Many scholars have dismissed this as essentially a wandering bender, because he spent so much time in country pubs, playing fiddle with local musicians, learning their tunes and turns-of-phrase.

But Burns made his populist intent exquisitely clear, naming the horse he bought for the trip Jenny Geddes, after a 17th-century Scottish woman who threw a stool at a bishop as he was announcing new religious rules from England's King Charles. The incident sparked a series of events that led to the English Civil War and the brief overthrow of the monarchy. Burns could not have been more clear about what he was rejecting – and what he was embracing.

He filled notebooks with examples of local slang and song and sketches of wildlife and plants. How does a fisherman describe a stormy day? How does a milkmaid describe a sunny day? He wanted people to feel that his songs came from someone who knew them – because he wanted his songs to become *their* songs.

"Most people who worked with folk songs in that day did an absolutely horrible job, because they didn't understand that the frankness and simplicity is the magic of it," says impressionistic Illinois songwriter Andrew Calhoun, who is working on contemporary renderings of Burns for a book and CD. "Burns was able to take a one-verse fragment and write seven beautiful verses that immediately became part of the folk tradition. Because he was not looking in from the outside; he was of the tradition, and yet had this incredibly developed literary skill."

Burns wrote charming but forceful letters to his publishers, who often wanted him to write more like the successful Romantic poet he had been.

Burns replied with vital lessons in the differences between a poem and a lyric, an art song and a popular song.

One publisher complained about him repeating a particular line so many times. Burns wrote back, "There is a peculiar rhythmus in many of our airs, and a necessity of adapting syllables to the emphasis, or what I call the feature notes of the tune, that cramp the poet and lay him under almost insuperable difficulties ... I might give you something more profound, yet it might not suit the light-horse gallop of the air so well as this random clink."

The publisher saw only the poem on the printed page. Burns saw a song, the needs of the melody – and of the singer. He would often call his wife, Jean Armour Burns, over to try out new verses. He called her the finest natural singer he'd ever heard, and she was his first singer. He would grill her: *Did that word halt in your throat? Did you have to rush that phrase? Were the vowels in the right place for your breathing?* Melding the right note to the right word was crucial to Burns, and no songwriter did it better.

Maureen McMullen is a trained singer equally at home with orchestras or folk ensembles, singing Broadway standards or folk songs by Burns. She teaches voice at the Berklee College of Music and says she enjoys singing Burns' songs "because it's a nice big sing."

"[He gave us] lots of lovely phrasing and shaping that can be done." she says. "The lyrics sit so beautifully on the right melody notes. Here at Berklee, particularly in the songwriting department, we call that *prosody*, when you get that perfect storm of a lyric that feels and sits with how the melody moves, and the mood of the song. It's a natural journey that the singer takes with both the lyric and melody."

Burns strived for that prosody, meticulously marrying lyric with melody, meaning with mood. He wrote candidly about his songwriting process: "Until

I am compleat master of a tune, in my own singing (such as it is), I can never compose for it. My way is: I consider the poetic Sentiment, correspondent to my idea of the musical expression; then choose my theme; begin one Stanza; when that is composed, which is generally the most difficult part of the business, I walk out, sit down now & then, look out for objects in Nature around me that are in unison or harmony with the cogitations of my fancy & workings of my bosom; humming every now & then the air with the verses I have framed; when I feel my Muse beginning to jade, I retire to the solitary fireside of my study, & there commit my effusions to paper; swinging, at intervals, on the hind-legs of my elbow-chair, by way of calling forth my own critical strictures, as my pen goes on."

Alexander Wright – a visceral roots songwriter who works under the stage name 2Ton Bridge – carves his songs from utterly American sources: failing farms and crumbling small towns, sun-stained workers and stark landscapes. He says Burns is a big part of how he learned to do that so well.

"Burns' language was music," he says. "When you speak a Robert Burns poem, you can't help but sing it. That's just a rhythmic thing, a use of language, the consonants and vowels and the way he puts up different rhyme schemes. It makes you move. Like music, it exists on so many simultaneous levels, on the meaning of the words but also the sound and rhythm and where it's all coming from, the depth of who he was and the sincerity of the images. You somehow know there's nothing in there he has not experienced himself."

Poet vs. Songwriter

Annoyed with a publisher's insistence that he write in a more conventional poetic style, Burns wrote, "Give me leave to criticize your taste in the only thing in

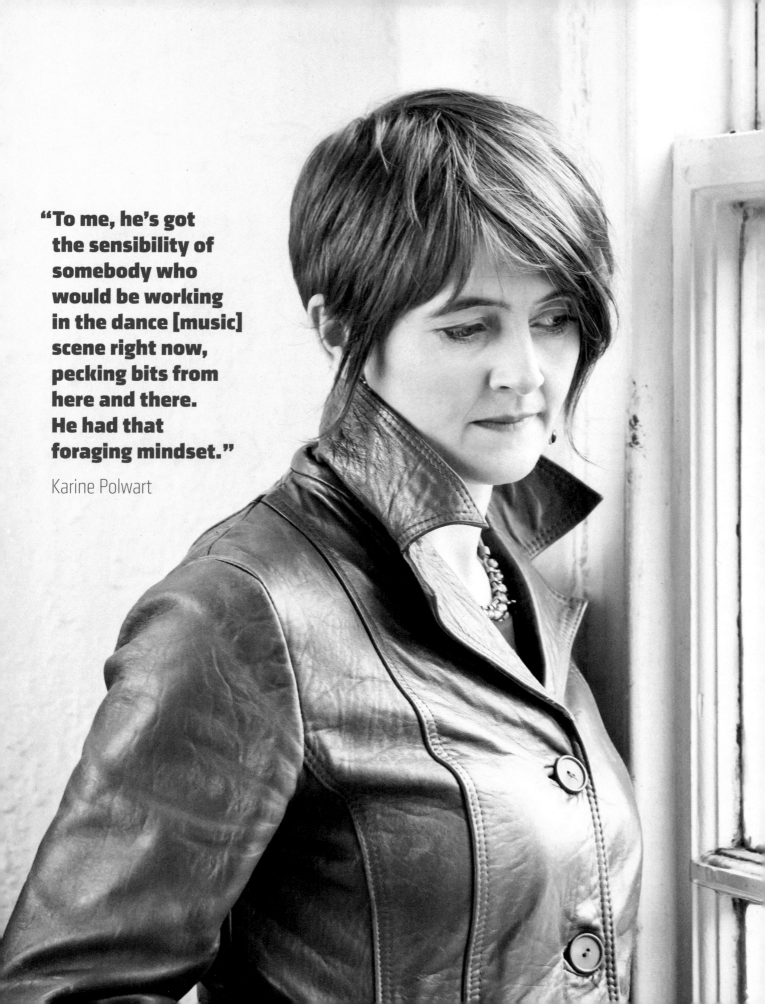

"To me, he's got the sensibility of somebody who would be working in the dance [music] scene right now, pecking bits from here and there. He had that foraging mindset."

Karine Polwart

which it is, in my opinion, reprehensible. You know I ought to know something of my own trade. Of pathos, sentiment and point you are a complete judge; but there is a quality more necessary than either in a song, and which is the very essence of a ballad; I mean simplicity."

In another letter, he predicted the honest values of the great folk songwriters who followed him, from Foster to Guthrie, the Carter Family to Steve Earle: "Originality is a coy feature in composition, and in a multiplicity of efforts in the same style, disappears. For these three thousand years we poetic folks have been describing the spring, for instance; and as the spring continues the same, there must soon be sameness in the imagery, etc, of these said rhyming folks."

Indeed, Burns never sought the obscure, artful image. Landscape was a crucial tool for him in evoking both place and emotion, but he always looked for the common image, the shared memory we could all see along with him. He believed, above all, in naturalness and authenticity. That's why he spent his later life traveling the Scottish countryside, seeing what his people saw, hearing what they heard. So he could get it right, and his vision could become theirs.

For Burns, as for the best of his musical descendants, there was only one way to ensure your song rings true: make it true.

He was once asked to evaluate a flowery faux-folk song with a line about a nightingale singing in a tree on the banks of the River Dee. Nice rhyme. Burns was furious. "In the first place," he wrote, "the nightingale sings in a low bush, but never from a tree; and in the second place, there never was a nightingale seen, or heard, on the banks of the Dee, or on the banks of any other river in Scotland."

"There's such a connection with place and landscape in Burns' songs, not only in the imagery but the way people inhabit the place they live," says Karine Polwart.

"My favorite of all his songs is 'Now, Westlin Winds' [also known as 'Song Composed in August']. It's amazing that he can write something that works like a love song, but is also a very modern ecology song – the whole philosophy of human co-existence with the planet – and a total shot at the leisure class, the hunting class. And just that one line, 'tyrannic man's dominion,' covers so much about how people either abuse or co-exist happily with the world around them. There's so much depth in his songs that stand up to new contexts, new ideas, and new dramas affecting the world."

One reason for Burns' subtlety in expressing politics was its danger in 18th-century Scotland. Burns was nearly tried for sedition several times. His best-known political song, "A Man's a Man for a' That," radically discounts the aristocracy, elevating the poor, honest man in its place. In an age of kings, men were hanged for less.

> *Give fools their silks, and knaves*
> *their wine,*
> *A man's a man for a' that*
> *Their tinsel show, an' a' that,*
> *The honest man, tho' e'er sae poor,*
> *Is king of men for a' that.*

Of course, that song was enormously popular in America. In 1849, abolitionist leader Frederick Douglass was invited to speak at an event honoring Burns, because his love for the poet was so well known, and he began, "Though I am no Scotchman and have colored skin, I am proud to be among you this evening." He pointed to a portrait of Burns, and said: "If any of you think me out of place at this occasion, I beg you lay the blame at the door of him who taught me that 'A Man's a Man for a' That.'"

Of Burns' populism and disdain for the ruling class, Polwart says, "[He] was in with all the movers and shakers of the day, all the great thinkers and writers and scientists were his circle, and then he walked away from all that. There was

an element of danger about many of his political ideas that made him an unwanted figure in those circles. You have to remember he was writing just ahead of the French Revolution. All those republican ideas are fomenting at that time, and are at the core of so many of his songs. That populist sensibility was seen as very dangerous."

His outspoken support for the American Revolution didn't help, either. In 1794, he wrote a poem celebrating George Washington's birthday:

> *But come ye sons of Liberty*
> *Columbia's offspring, brave as free,*
> *In danger's hour still flaming*
> *in the van,*
> *Ye know, & dare maintain,*
> *The Royalty of Man.*

He actually concludes by saying these American rebels are the true royalty of the world. And Burns was surely aware, as were those he'd insulted, that the radicals who started the American Revolution called themselves the Sons Of Liberty. All this greatly enhanced his superstar status in the new American republic.

Personal Politics

Burns traced his radical populism to early childhood: "Almost the earliest thing I do remember, when I was quite a boy, one day at church, being enraged at seeing … one of the maids of his house, rise from the mouth of the pew to give way to a bloated son of Wealth & Dullness, who waddled surlily past her. Indeed, the girl was very pretty; and he was an ugly, stupid, purse-proud, money-loving old monster."

Because Burns wrote from so deeply within the lives of ordinary people, many of his political songs still hold up, just like the populist songs of Guthrie or Seeger. Scottish harpist-singer Maeve Gilchrist, who also teaches at Berklee, says, "Burns managed to write the most perfect political songs, because they're so beautifully framed. His imagery is so stunning, his descriptions of the landscape and nature so beautifully interwoven with these poetic references to social justice and politics. A lot of songwriters I know tend to stay far away from political writing, because they think a political song can't be a beautiful song as well. Burns is a wonderful representation of a beautiful songwriter at surface level, and a deep thinker and philosopher at second glance. And able to do both seamlessly."

Burns' egalitarianism did have its limits, though. One night he was snowbound in a small inn, forced to listen to a horrible country fiddler. In a letter to a friend, he wrote, "Since dinner, a scraper has been torturing catgut, in sounds that would have insulted the dying agonies of a sow under the hands of a butcher, and thinks himself, on that very account, exceeding good company."

He added that he was debating whether to solve the problem by drinking heavily or committing suicide. "I, of two evils," he concluded, "have chosen the least, and am very drunk, at your service."

What modern folk music fan or musician hasn't been *there* a few times?

Because Burns wrote so authentically about real people's lives, his best political songs still feel relevant. Says Red House Records' Eric Peltoniemi, "When [Burns] writes about poor men forced to be soldiers, because their old rural lives are vanishing, he could be writing about small-town America in the 21st century."

Still, during Burns' lifetime, attempts were made to gentrify the populist folk bard that Americans loved so deeply. Composers Ludwig van Beethoven, George Handel, and Ignaz Pleyel were commissioned to create prim classical settings for his songs. Burns fiercely fought their attempts to classicize the old folk melodies.

"Whatever Mr. Pleyel does," he wrote to a publisher, "let him not alter one iota of the original Scottish airs ... but let

our national music preserve its native features. They are, I own, frequently wild and irreducible to the more modern rules; but on that very eccentricity, perhaps, depends a great part of their effect."

Andrew Calhoun says that when Burns complained about the complexity of Beethoven's arrangements, the great composer sniffed, "I do not write for children."

Over time, this gentrified Burns came to overshadow the radical fiddler-poet in the minds of most Americans. "Culture made Burns stuffier than he ever would have liked," says the Library of Congress' Nancy Groce. "It was a bowdlerized and increasingly gentrified Burns that emerged in Victorian times – but that's not the Burns that early America embraced."

A New Burnsian Folk Revival

In the last 15 years, there's been an epic Burns revival in Scotland, liberating him from his confinement as the stiff-collared icon on shortbread tins and tea cozies. He is being embraced by folk and pop musicians, hailed as Scotland's Woody Guthrie, not its Shakespeare.

"There's been a reconnection with a much broader sense of his repertoire, and all his songs have finally been recorded," says Karine Polwart, referring to the 12-CD *Complete Songs of Robert Burns* released in 2007 on Alliance Records, arranged by Burns scholar Fred Freeman and performed in a spare folk style by Scottish musicians like Polwart, Jim Malcolm, Janet Russell, Ed Miller, and the late Tony Cuffe, who helped inspire the revival with his sweet, savvy Burns covers in the landmark Scottish band Ossian.

"That collection has had a big impact on the Scottish folk scene," Polwart adds. "[It has] brought tons of songs back into currency that hadn't been sung for a long time. And the part of his repertoire that's been overlooked is the part where he was

preserving fiddle and pipe tunes by setting his words to them."

That revival has not really taken hold in the US, even though Burns was such a foundational voice in the development of our music and literature. As the Victorian image of Burns came to overshadow the actual man, he became the province of ritualized Burns suppers, formal recitals, and bekilted Vaudeville tenors.

Aengus Finan is a lilting Canadian songwriter whose style is best described as Canadiana – North American roots spiced with Celtic tang instead of Southern twang. But he is better known as the director of Folk Alliance International, a vibrant trade organization for the modern folk world. "I think the missing element for that greater adoption of his Guthrie-level place within the folk community here, as a resource and a benchmark, is how long the footsteps are to get there," he says. "You have to roll up your sleeves to appreciate Burns, wrestle with some of the dialect.

"When I got past that," he adds, "it struck me how much potential there was in writing about the day-to-day, street-level, intimate moments of life. I didn't feel like his songs were about him; they were about everybody. That rang true for me: how do I make this universal; how do I get past my view of the topic? Burns is a model for that."

Other folk songwriters in the States have found the same modern lessons in Burns, from that sweeping universality to the technical nitty-gritty of writing songs that matter to ordinary people.

Diana Jones, who was an adopted child, began her career as a roots music songwriter when she sought out the culture of her birth family. Hearing her grandfather sing Appalachian folk songs, she felt something primal stir in her blood – Burns' songs were beloved by the first Scots-Irish settlers in Appalachia. In Burns, Jones heard the roots of her roots music and the rudiments for the honestly hewn, real-life songs she writes

"Burns is all about looking for the dignity in every person, every action, every gesture. ... [His work is] about taking that world that's so small and unnoticed – and lifting it up for the world to see."

Alexander Wright (2Ton Bridge)

so well, and sings beautifully, on her *Live in Concert* album, which released this February. Guthrie would have felt right at home with Jones.

"One thing I love about Burns," she says, "is that he's not afraid of reinforcing core ideas through repetition. And it's fun for people to sing something over and over, go off on these verse journeys, but keep being brought back to the house. Burns' stuff is all so air-tight that way. So for younger writers, especially, it's great to go back to those very beautiful, very well-written songs that are so simple – but deceptively so."

As 2Ton Bridge, Alexander Wright is another Americana songwriter who learned the right lessons from Burns, especially in the uncompromising yet kind-eyed songs he writes about the dispossessed of our heedless culture. He never condescends to the hard-hit people in his songs, but pays them same respect Burns did: to see other people as they see themselves. His music is as American as the last dirt road you traveled, rippling with the sinewy groove of worked muscles.

"Burns is all about looking for the dignity in every person, every action, every gesture," Wright says. "So when I write about a post-hole digger – '35 years laying out fence/ It all lines up but it don't make sense' – or a farmer telling the government to take its hands off his land, I'm trying to capture the heroism and dignity of everyday life. And Burns did that all the time. I mean, who else would write a whole poem about a louse he sees on a lady's hat in church? It's about taking that world that's so small and unnoticed – and lifting it up for the world to see."

Polwart cites the breadth of Burns' subject matter as "a massive source of inspiration. It's tempting to go down a little cul-de-sac as a songwriter, writing one kind of song, and Burns was leaping across so many types. He wrote dance music, drinking songs, bawdy songs, love songs, narrative ballads, political satire, work songs. There aren't many songwriters willing to do that today."

Songwriters today might also learn from how well Burns wrote for other singers. "There's a natural ebb and flow to Burns that's a joy for a singer," says Berklee's Maureen McMullen, "because the way the lyric is written feels authentic to the emotion associated with it. We talk about songs having a 'golden spot.' Typically, that's about three-quarters of the way through a line, so there's a tension, a peak, and then a trough. And that peak is the golden spot. But some of Burns' songs have a golden spot all the way through, or what you might call a sub-golden spot. In 'Ae Fond Kiss,' the two highest pitches are on 'heart' and 'farewell.' That's no accident – it's exactly what the song is about."

According to Andrew Calhoun, today's folk songwriters could also take a cue from how Burns used traditional melodies. "Burns set lyrics to existing folk melodies," he says. "Very few writers create melodies that interesting; I know I don't. Sometimes Burns would take a fast tune, slow it down and find interesting things in it, then make a new song."

That certainly influenced Woody Guthrie, who liked to brag that "I never wrote an original melody on purpose." In 1947, Guthrie wrote an open letter called "To That Man Robert Burns." The Dust Bowl Troubadour marveled at the vastness of the Ploughman Poet's legacy:

Your words turned into songs and floated upstream and then turned into rains and drifted down and lodged and swung and clung to drifts of driftwood to warm and heat and fertilize new seeds.

As if commiserating with someone like Guthrie from the other side of history, a 25-year-old Robert Burns wrote a letter to a friend, enclosing a song he'd just written. In it, he sounds like any honest young songwriter today, wondering if the heart and wonder he feels within his new song could possibly enter the hearts and wonder of others. He had no idea what his songs would mean to the world, especially to a place called the United States of America that was still struggling to be born.

"As I have been all along, a miserable dupe to Love," Burns wrote, "and have been led into a thousand weaknesses and follies by it, for that reason I put the more confidence in my critical skill in distinguishing foppery and conceit, from real passion and nature. Whether to say the following song will stand the test, I will not pretend to say, because it is my own; only I can say it was, at the time, *real.*"

When Diana Jones hears that, she laughs softly, but for a long time. Finally, almost in a whisper, she says, "You know, I think I have a new epitaph for my tombstone. I want it to say, 'It was, at the time, real.'" ■

VIRGINIA IS FOR (MUSIC) LOVERS

Along the Commonwealth's Crooked Road, Dori Freeman makes a storybook connection

by Mike Seely

IN NOVEMBER 2014, THE GREAT second-generation singer-songwriter Teddy Thompson – son of Richard and Linda – received an unsolicited message via Facebook from a 23-year-old woman who was living with her boyfriend and infant daughter in tiny Ellijay, Georgia. The message contained a recording of the young woman singing a simple, elegant waltz she'd written, titled "Lullaby."

Thompson says that typically when he listens to music from aspiring artists, it's "almost always awful and often funny." The frequency with which he's sent unknown music that captures his interest is "never." And, he adds, "Unless you're totally delusional, most people realize it's not going to work."

But this tune was different. "It took me maybe 10 to 12 seconds to realize she's great," Thompson says of his reaction to the voice of Dori Freeman, now 24 and raising her two-year-old alone in her native Galax, Virginia, a Blue Ridge Parkway town of some 7,000 residents. "As surprised as I was to find something good in that arena," Thompson says, "I was instantly on board."

He told her to send him more tracks. "I realized she had a whole album of really good songs, and I said, 'Let's make a record.' I was going to be in Nashville a couple months after we were corresponding, so I suggested meeting up to make sure we didn't dislike each other. Unless something terrible happened, we were already on track to make a record."

Nothing terrible happened, and three months after Freeman sought out Thompson on Facebook, the two were in a New York studio cutting her self-titled debut, which was financed entirely through $12,000 raised from donors on Kickstarter. With Thompson serving as producer, the record was released in February to instant acclaim. Of their collaboration, Thompson says, "I didn't really do anything other than put a microphone in front of her. She just got up there and sang everything pretty much live. The thing I liked the most about her is that, in sharp contrast to most things these days, there's very little decoration. Even people who play traditional music have been so influenced with the American Idol-ization of everything, that's it's painful for me to listen to. She's in the Carter Family or Iris Dement aesthetic – maybe a little Gillian Welch. Their approach to singing and writing is quite similar – that straight-to-the-heart delivery."

In spite of her storybook connection with Thompson, Freeman has, in a way, been bred for this moment all her life. She comes from a family of musicians revered along Virginia's Crooked Road, a seminal roots-music trail of 60 venues and festivals that was formally recognized in 2003. Every week, her dad Scott, an elite fiddler, and grandpa Willard play to rapt audiences at the family-owned Front Porch Gallery and Frame Shop in Galax, and Freeman only missed the town's 80-year-old Old Fiddlers' Convention the year her daughter was born.

"I grew up surrounded by bluegrass and old-time and folk and blues," she says – and in her neck of the woods, she's hardly alone.

Never Seen So Much Music

Although its music has existed since America's inception, the 330-mile Crooked Road's name was coined 13 years ago by folklorist Joe Wilson and a community developer named Todd Christensen.

Jack Hinshelwood is the director of Heartwood, a multimillion-dollar arts facility in Abingdon, Virginia, that features a state-of-the-art performance hall and hosts its own three-day music festival. "Joe, from his encyclopedic knowledge about this kind of music, knew that there were some pretty unique

"Any family you talk to will have somebody who plays music, and now the kids are taking it up and playing and taking it in a little different direction – like Mumford & Sons and that kind of style. But they're still learning in the same tradition as their mom or dad and grandparents learned."

Scott Freeman

music venues, such as the Carter Family Fold in Bristol, Tennessee," says Hinshelwood, who notes that there are nine major music venues on the Crooked Road, as well as dozens of smaller places to play. "And they said, 'Let's connect these with a heritage music driving trail called the Crooked Road, so that visitors could envision not just coming for one day but for a week or two, to explore this region where people have kept this music for hundreds of years.'"

"This music" is of a decidedly down-home variety, with bluegrass at its core and dancing on the floor.

"It originated in these Appalachian mountains – Irish, English and Scottish people that settled this area hundreds of years ago brought their fiddles with them," says Wayne Henderson, a self-described "hillbilly picker" and luthier who's crafted custom guitars for the likes of Eric Clapton, Vince Gill, Doc Watson, and Gillian Welch.

"Clawhammer banjo and fiddle – that's the kind of music around here mostly," he adds. "Slaves from Africa brought banjos with them. We think that's where old-time music came from, and that's always been a big part of life in southwest Virginia, northwest [North] Carolina, and northeast Tennessee. Flat-foot dancing was one of the main forms of entertainment because people were not well-to-do and couldn't travel anywhere, so they'd roll up the rug and have a big dance."

"These traditional music forms are not static by any means," adds Hinshelwood. "What we have here is a real diversity of musical forms – everything from ballad singing, Carter Family music, great guitar music, old-time stringbands, bluegrass, jug bands, gospel quartet singing. When you hear Ralph Stanley sing, you're hearing the echoes of the primitive Baptist church."

Five years ago, Hinshelwood set out to produce a two-CD compilation of 50 current musicians who lived along the Crooked Road. He put out a call for submissions, and among hundreds he received was one from Dori Freeman, whose father Hinshelwood was well acquainted with. Upon playing her disc in his car stereo, Hinshelwood experienced a Thompson-esque epiphany.

"I heard like two songs before I pulled off the road and called Scott and said, 'Holy shit, I cannot believe I haven't heard about your daughter,'" Hinshelwood recalls. "We used her version of Cannonball Adderley's 'Work Song' on the CD. She has a voice and a sensibility that is so far beyond her years that it just blows me away."

While practice makes perfect, Freeman's granddad Willard Gayheart concedes, "She has genes on both sides, so I guess it was just inevitable where she would want to go." Hinshelwood takes things a step further, noting that the Freeman-Gayheart clan "could be almost like poster children for what the

Crooked Road means, which is music that is kept in families over generations and passed down."

Gayheart grew up in the mountains of Kentucky – "way back in the sticks," as he puts it. When he moved to Galax, he'd "never seen so much music being played" anywhere in his life. While he'd dabbled in guitar as a Bluegrass State youngster, he immersed himself upon settling in Virginia.

A revered pencil artist who's published three sketchbooks of renderings of Appalachian life, Gayheart's frame shop features both his art and a Friday-night music showcase where he strives "to showcase the better musicians from around the area" before an audience of 40 to 50 patrons. But they don't come much better than Gayheart and Freeman's dad, a fiddler and mandolinist who teaches music lessons out of the shop for a living.

Scott Freeman, who grew up across the North Carolina border in Mount Airy, had a granddad who played banjo and a dad who loved to flat-foot dance (like Irish dancing, infused with a barn-floor sensibility). Scott, who often accompanies his pupils – he instructs more than 40 per week – onstage at the Old Fiddlers' Convention, describes his family's existence on the Crooked Road like so: "We have these beautiful, green, rolling hills in the summertime, close to the New River. It's a beautiful place to live and raise a family. Great food – fried

> **"I was brought up here and have spent the better part of my adult life here. I feel an incredible bond to this part of the country. The people here are some of the most straightforward, sincere people you could ever want to know."**
>
> Dori Freeman

squash in the summertime is always a great meal, homegrown tomatoes. Any family you talk to will have somebody who plays music, and now the kids are taking it up and playing and taking it in a little different direction – like Mumford & Sons and that kind of style. But they're still learning in the same tradition as their mom or dad and grandparents learned."

A Gorgeous Voice, Tied to the Land

Wayne Henderson has received a National Heritage Award, toured alongside Jerry Douglas and Albert Lee, and given concerts at Carnegie Hall. On the third Saturday of every June, he hosts an eponymous music festival and guitar competition in Mouth of Wilson, Virginia, that Freeman considers herself fortunate to have played and attended.

The admiration, it turns out, is mutual. "She's one of my favorites," says Henderson of Freeman. "She has a gorgeous voice. I can't help but think people who try hard and have natural talent might amount to something."

Around the time Freeman first picked up a guitar at the age of 15, she took a shine to the music of Rufus Wainwright and, in turn, his longtime friend Thompson. "[Teddy] was the only

person I reached out to," says the petite, strawberry-blonde Freeman of her long-shot Facebook message. "I've been a huge fan of Teddy's for a really long time."

When Freeman and Thompson got together, he says she wanted him to sing on the record "as much as possible." Ultimately, he agreed to lend harmonies to three ballads – "Where I Stood," "Any Wonder," and "A Song for Paul" – which, probably not by coincidence, are the album's strongest tracks. Here, Freeman's voice is languid and dreamy, with hints of Patty Griffin, Norah Jones, and Zoe Muth. But she's got a spunkier side as well: "Tell Me" is a punchy, witty affair that recalls Lydia Loveless, where Freeman's voice produces a blissful, triple-hitched yodel effect on the word "man" that's apt to make a woman take her dress in her fingertips, tilt her head toward the sun and spin around barefoot in the grass like a 2-year-old.

Speaking of which, Freeman's daughter "really likes to dance to anything." As Mom ponders how aggressively to tour behind her album (a stint supporting Thompson, who has his own new LP out this spring, is under consideration), single-parenting poses a delicate quandary.

"That's a tricky one," she concedes. "I want to be able to tour and play my music live, but also want to sacrifice as little time away from my daughter as

possible. I think it's just something I'll have to navigate as it happens. Of course, I would love to take her with me whenever possible."

If she can't, Freeman says she's "lucky to have a really supportive and helpful family, immediate and extended," back home in Galax to look after her offspring. Yet while Freeman would love to have the sort of career Kacey Musgraves has forged, don't expect her to emulate that small-town Texas girl's move to Nashville. Freeman's an Appalachian artist through and through, and couldn't be more proud to call Galax home.

"I was brought up here and have spent the better part of my adult life here," she says. "I feel an incredible bond to this part of the country. The people here are some of the most straightforward, sincere people you could ever want to know. The backbone of Appalachia is built on generations of hard-working folks who were tied to the land in an almost literal sense, in that they depended on the land for so much of their survival. I think that's why the music of this region is so easily identifiable as being Appalachian, because it's so bound to the hearts and souls of the people here. And I truly hope that some of the younger torch-bearers of this music, myself included, can erase some of the stereotypes that people sadly still hold today about Appalachia." ∎

ROOM TO WANDER

**Willy Vlautin's
persistent portrait
of the Western drifter**

by Gwendolyn Elliott

WILLY VLAUTIN RENTS AN OFFICE the size of a small bedroom in the St. Johns neighborhood of Portland, Oregon, where he works at a desk that faces north. Inside the room is another window to the west, a mustard-colored vintage sofa on the opposite wall, a cozy electric heater, his guitar, and a small collection of personal keepsakes that include a Willie Nelson poster by local artist Gary Houston, set memorabilia from *The Motel Life* – a film based on his first novel – and two black-and-white photos of Hollywood starlets Carole Lombard and Myrna Loy. A few oversize posters are tacked to the wall, but most everything else either leans on the wall or lives in a neat pile on the floor.

This is the place Vlautin, a songwriter who has released 10 studio albums with his alt-country band, Richmond Fontaine, and a novelist with four published tomes to his name, suggests for a chat. Its sparse decor also suggests something else: Vlautin, like so many of his characters in song and on the page, doesn't seem to know how long he's going to stay.

Granted, he's been here for just over a year, having relocated workspaces from elsewhere in the neighborhood. But the setup is interesting indeed for one long-fascinated with the spirit of the drifter.

Old-Man Bars

Growing up in Reno with his brother and single mom, Vlautin says his interest in drifting took root, for better or worse, early on. "My dad was a lawyer, but he left when I was two," he explains.

His mom was a secretary whose boss "would find guys off the Truckee River, these kind of homeless guys, and [he] would try to save them. She worked with a revolving door with these guys who would clean themselves up and then fall apart."

Vlautin, 48, has been living in and around Portland for over 20 years and now lives in Scappoose – a small town about a half-hour's drive from the city. He has a friendly face and speaks with a twangy, conversational drawl. On the day he has me over to his office, he's wearing work boots, jeans, a button-up flannel shirt, and a Carhartt jacket. It's all utilitarian wear not entirely out of place in the Portland neighborhood where he works, a historically working class area in some places still untouched by the march of gentrification that's seized the city practically everywhere else.

"I told my girlfriend if they kill Slim's and the Wishing Well and Marie's – those three bars, those are the last three Reno bars – then I'll have to move," he says. "I can't live in a place without an old-man bar."

The origins of his worldview, in fact, began in a bar like that. "Reno had a lot of drifter men," he says. "Around 17, 18, I started sneaking into old-man bars, just to see what it was like. You want to see … the guy with three fingers. I always liked that stuff because it made me feel normal. I felt easier when I was in a room full of freaks or failed people, so I romanticized it. But I was young, so when you're young, and you're hanging out with a 40-year-old alcoholic guy who might have half his face caved in because he got in a car wreck, because he was drunk, or he'd been married, twice, or his kid had died, it seems kind of romantic, like he's already lived. It wasn't until I was about 30 that I realized these guys just lived in a bar, they haven't done anything."

The True Things

Vlautin's books and albums are almost exclusively cast with such characters. Down on their luck brothers Jerry Lee and Frank of *The Motel Life* round a vicious cycle of illness, poverty, and crime. Their accidental brushes with good luck are inevitably trumped by their own bad decisions. *Lean on Pete*'s 15-year-old Charley loses his neglectful father and falls in with seedy figures from the low-level racetrack Portland Meadows. Walter Denny is a recurring character on the 2003 Southwest-themed album *Post to Wire,* who dispatches postcards (as Vlautin-voiced spoken-word vignettes) from a life on the lam.

The American West has long been fitted for these types of stories, and it's a device Vlautin works hard. The West is, after all, the final frontier for the American drifter, the backdrop for figures in the American music, poetry, literature, and film peddled by Johnny

Cash, Merle Haggard, Utah Phillips, Jimmie Rodgers, Ramblin' Jack Elliott, the Sons of the Pioneers, John Prine, Guy Clark, Willie Nelson, Bob Dylan, Woody Guthrie, Townes Van Zandt, Raymond Carver, John Steinbeck, Ken Kesey, Jack Kerouac, and Gus Van Sant, just for starters.

"Life centers around who you get a ride from, where you spend the night, how much money you have in your pocket. There are no long-range plans," wrote Roger Ebert in a 1991 review of Van Sant's Portland-based hustler drama, *My Own Private Idaho,* which could easily stand in for *The Motel Life*. Like Van Sant, a famous Portland resident, Vlautin filters a lot of his work through the gray, low cloud cover of the Pacific Northwest, using the region's rivers, warehouses, and industrial sites as the inspiration for his songs: "Willamette," "Glisan Street," and "Montgomery Park," to name a few.

He likes to follow his imagination outside of Oregon, too, dipping his peripatetic subjects in and out of other Western states like Wyoming, Nevada, Colorado, Arizona, California, and Washington.

"I always wanted to write true stories, or what I think is true," he says, explaining that his ideas are inspired less by his own experiences, and more by inventions of feeling. "I write about the true things that hurt me or I can't figure out, the things that scarred me up or put a dent in me, things that wake you up in the middle of the night worrying. I write about those."

Vlautin also writes in overlapping cycles, returning to the same hotspots again and again: A troubled soul like Allison Johnson, the battered girlfriend protagonist of his second novel, *Northline,* is also the name of a song on *Post to Wire*. Echoing the novel of the same name, "Northline" is also a track from his 2002 album, *Winnemucca.* Denver's Colfax Avenue is the stage for a dramatic scene in *Lean on Pete,* as well as the name of the first album of his side project, the Delines, and the subject of the song, "Kid from Belmont Street gets Left on Colfax St. Denver, CO." The Vegas casino "El Cortez" doubles as a song and the name of Vlautin's record label.

The characters, places, and references drift across his albums and books with such frequency that

the songwriter and novelist has essentially created his own mythology. Though it's a trail of breadcrumbs that almost always leads to a fork in the road, setting the cycle into motion again.

Vlautin began writing stories, he says, "because I was trying to find a world I wanted to live in," and indeed he's created that world.

Beginning of an Ending

As we sit chatting in an office – not a practice space or studio – I have to wonder whether Vlautin is ready to focus exclusively on his novels.

"I guess it just depends on what's doing better at the time," he says. "When I'm writing a novel that's not working, then I think of myself as a musician; when I'm not writing good tunes, or the band aren't doing good, then I think of myself as a writer. I write most of my songs here, too."

Vlautin shares Richmond Fontaine with an ensemble of some of the Rose City's most versatile and enduring players. Along with his vocals, which have long drawn comparisons to Jay Farrar, the lonesome whistle of Paul Brainard's pedal steel – which has also appeared on albums by M. Ward, Bobby Bare Jr., and Alejandro Escovedo – helped establish the group's distinctive alt-country sound.

These days, Fontaine is filled out with Dan Eccles on guitar, longtime drummer Sean Oldham, and Jenny Conlee-Drizos (Decemberists) on keys. The latter two, along with bassist Freddy Trujillo, also play in Vlautin's other group, the Delines. (Sisters and vocalists Amy Boone and Deborah Kelly of the Damnations round out that band, a sultry lounge-noir act with a vibe somewhere between Tom Waits and Mazzy Star.)

Orbiting these projects, Vlautin has also scored a soundtrack (the documentary *A Fighting Heart,* about the Irish Boxer Johnny Kilbane) with longtime friend and Delines/Fontaine producer John Askew; seen *The Motel Life* transformed into a film starring Kris Kristofferson; nabbed numerous book awards, including the Nevada Silver Pen Award (*The Motel Life*) and the Ken Kesey Award for Fiction (*Lean On Pete*); and is currently working on his fifth novel,

> "I always wanted to write true stories, or what I think is true. I write about the true things that hurt me or I can't figure out, the things that scarred me up or put a dent in me."
>
> Willy Vlautin

which he calls "a big sprawling modern-day Western about failing ranches."

Fontaine has been steady through it all, though it has accumulated a much bigger following abroad, in the UK and Australia. "My band never did that good for years, and we're still a small-time band," he says. "We'd have ups and downs, people would say you sucked and people would say they liked you. Some people would leave and others would drive ten hours to see you. It's all over the map. ... We were pals first, and never really good business guys, and we weren't ambitious except we wanted to make records and things."

When talk turns to the band's recently released tenth full-length record, *You Can't Go Back If There's Nothing To Go Back To* (March 18, Fluff and Gravy Records), Vlautin says that though his songwriting career elsewhere is still going strong, his work with Fontaine might soon be drawing to a close.

He shows me a small painting on canvas by the window across from his desk – an oil work by Nevada artist Greg Allen that Fontaine used for the cover of *You Can't Go Back*. It depicts a horse

standing alone in the desert, its head leaning low, just slightly toward the viewer. The perspective is from some distance off, but Vlautin shows me the photo that inspired it.

"I was driving around central Nevada," he says, "me and this friend of mine, and we were about 40 miles from paved road, and we came across this blind horse. You can't really tell from here, but its eyes had rotted out, and it was really intense to look at. We're standing there, and it's in the desert, there's a cattle water trough about a half mile from there, but he can't walk anywhere, he doesn't know what he's doing. I was looking at him, and I just noticed all his scars, and he was finished, he was fucking dead. I started thinking about that in terms of ... Richmond Fontaine, because we're kind of coming to our end, too."

Writing Workhorse

Vlautin talked a lot about horses this day. Like his reappearing characters and scenes, the image comes up elsewhere in his metaphors: "I'm not that prolific," he

says, when I ask about his output. "I'm just kind of a workhorse."

He talks about his struggle with horse track gambling. "I love the track, and the track was starting to hurt me, and I was starting to meet people on the backside of the track, and asking, 'What happened to this horse, or that horse?'" He also talks about his connection with his girlfriend, Lee, a "horsewoman," and their three retired racehorses. And so on.

For a man of his particular vocation, it makes for another allegory: horses are a symbol of the freedom to roam, one long associated with the West. "I always wanted to write about the West," Vlautin says, before adding, "I don't have any idea – musically or [with my] writing – if anything I've done means anything."

But Vlautin can't stop chasing tumbleweeds into the sunset. Writing, he says, is his way of keeping one step ahead of the drifter in him.

"It's my favorite thing to do," he says. I was always like, 'After my next failed project I'm going to quit,' but I'd always have another one in the works, so then I'd say, 'I'm going to quit after my next book,' but then I'd already have one in the works, so I don't want to quit on this one." ∎

SOME-THING NEW IN THE WATER

**Pokey LaFarge feels
a change coming on**

by Cat Johnson

IT'S MID-AFTERNOON AND POKEY LaFarge hasn't eaten yet. He's on his couch in St. Louis, surrounded by notebooks. The singer-songwriter has been drinking coffee all day, trying to make sense of his notes. One of the books contains completed songs; the others are home to diary entries, song ideas, potential lyrics, to-do lists, and notes about "the sonic nature of a specific song."

"I guess you could say the hope is that they lead to a finished product," LaFarge says over the phone, explaining that he wishes he had a way to make the system more organized. "Every artist I've ever known has piles of notes."

Something Missing

Born Andrew Heissler in Bloomington, Illinois, in 1983, LaFarge was an early convert to American roots music. He discovered it as a youngster – while other kids around him were listening to Snoop Dogg and Ice Cube, he was listening to Skip James and Sleepy John Estes. In these areas of roots music, he found something deeper. In a previous interview, he told me that the older music had qualities he felt were missing from what was on the radio.

His exploration of early American styles led him to guitar and banjo, and he

has made a career of it. With his focus on under-appreciated roots styles, he's a standout among contemporary artists, and has introduced early 20th-century roots music to countless fans who, like LaFarge, may seek something more timeless than the latest pop hit.

Since 2006, when he released his debut, *Marmalade*, LaFarge has been one of the few artists outside of underground roots circles to showcase that midcentury musical sweet spot where early jazz, country, swing, and the blues all swirled around to create something exciting and absolutely American.

In 2010, Jack White heard him on WSM 650 AM, home of the Grand Ole Opry, and invited him to record for Third Man Records. The resulting 7-inch single, *Chittlin' Cookin' Time in Cheatham County*, which was released in 2011, and a self-titled EP in 2013 – as well as 16 tour dates opening for White – catapulted LaFarge into the international spotlight.

LaFarge says his time with Third Man was "certainly good for business," as he grew his audience to include the indie rock crowd. Indeed, from the broader platform of Third Man, he turned countless young people on to the music that formed the pre-rock and roll foundation for much of what is popular today.

Citing Milton Brown & His Musical Brownies, Roy Newman & His Boys, the Mississippi Sheiks, and the Skillet Lickers as a few of his key influences, LaFarge's catalog is full of punchy lyrics about pretty girls, appreciating where you're from, enjoying life, being treated badly, and celebrating Midwestern culture. His sound has a rhythmic emphasis on the backbeat, tight cymbal snaps, horns and banjos playing together nicely, call and response with his backup singers, and an era-specific vibrato that one just doesn't hear much of these days. And, like some of the music he's inspired by, he leans in the direction of novelty without ever falling in or losing the integrity of a song.

The tune "Underground," from *Something in the Water* (released April 2015 on Rounder Records), for example, starts with drums and chanting that sounds right out of a tiki bar, but the lyrics paint a different story:

If there's a god, he's of the land
And he does not favor any man
Father time has the final say,
but it doesn't matter anyway
Mother Nature has made a deal
and now it's done.

"When Did You Leave Heaven," from the same album, is a swoon-inducing throwback to early crooners like Bing Crosby, but there's just enough of a Hank Williams edge to appeal to roots appreciators.

Now that he's perfected that sound – after years of touring and writing and growing a fanbase – he's finding it's time to develop a way to keep track of all his ideas. LaFarge is in what he describes as a very prolific time, writing more than ever. And what he's working on is not what anyone would expect.

"From what I can see of the plethora of material I have currently," he says, "my writing and its evolution is really just kind of exploding. The rhythm is changing, the grooves are changing, I'm seeing the grooves and sounds to be heavier, the drums and the bass to be heavier, and the horns to be more slammin', as opposed to swinging.

"You hear guys like Jason Isbell and other singer-songwriters, and the rhythm and the groove doesn't seem to matter to them all that much," he adds. "They're able to convey everything just with the words. I'm more interested in composers where the groove and the rhythms and the instrumental hooks are just as important as the lyrics."

LaFarge wants to move away from being limited to a certain genre or style of singing and songwriting. Among the artists he's currently gleaning inspiration from are Paul Simon, Warren Zevon,

"No matter how I express it, if it's a good song, it's a good song. And if it's my song, then it's me."

Pokey LaFarge

Roy Orbison, Neil Diamond, and Randy Newman. "For me," he says, "it's about making a beautiful composition, beautiful music, and really getting it into hearts."

Room to Grow

LaFarge has become more open-minded over the last couple of years, and his songwriting has flourished. But while he's given a lot of freedom to the musicians in his band, he doesn't feel like he's given himself enough freedom to let his songwriting shine – to be the person and the composer he wants to be. "I think maybe at times I was scared to write a certain song, or convey a certain feeling that I had, because I thought that it was too different from myself," he says. "I realized that, no matter what I'm feeling, [it's] right, and that needs to be communicated. No matter how I express it, if it's a good song, it's a good song. And if it's my song, then it's me."

With that epiphany, he's finding he needs to challenge himself to grow, and to challenge his audience to grow along with him – something with which he struggles. He questions whether he got too comfortable with what his sound was at one certain time. When asked if he's concerned about losing fans who know and love him as a traditional roots artist, LaFarge says that he's less traditional than some people think. The sentiment is puzzling because, from the outside, his commitment to early-20th century American styles has seemed all-consuming. With his slick, styled hair, newsboy features, wide ties, cuffed jeans, retro shirts and pants, and hat tipped to the side, LaFarge looks like he just rolled onto the stage from 75 years ago. Then he

opens his mouth and seals the deal with his Midwestern accent and charm, and lyrics that point to a time when cities like Chicago and St. Louis were epicenters of music and culture.

LaFarge admits that, as his traditional sensibilities become less obvious, some people may say he's abandoning them. But his desire to be free and open to possibilities is stronger than the pressure he feels to stay put stylistically. "The good people want to see me evolve," he says, "and they want me to grow."

So how does his appreciation of early American roots music inform this shift into more rhythm- and groove-focused songwriting? "The hope is that by being open to a wide array of ideas and grooves and themes and stories that I'm hearing in my head, that the foundation will never be lost," he says. "The hope is that it will be built upon and it will be stronger. I'm confident that that's already happening with some of the material I have."

Pulling Back

A veteran of the road, LaFarge has toured the world, acting as an informal ambassador of American roots music. But there are challenges to being on the road all the time, and he was looking forward to performing less this year, to focus on writing and recording. He estimated he'll play 50 shows, as compared to the 150 or 200 a year he's been playing for the better part of a decade. And he planned to start recording a new album this spring.

"I've been in such a grind for seven years," he says, "just pumping out records and touring. I just don't think that I've been able to do justice

to the emotions that come from the experiences I've had."

How the new record will sound remains to be seen, but, as when LaFarge first discovered country and blues, he is looking to the music to help him find his place in the world. "When I was younger, I was really unsure of myself," he says. "I had no sure idea about anything, but I had lots of ideas. I was just giving it all a shot. I wanted something that was raw and unfiltered, and straight from the source, so the early blues and the early country really touched me for that reason."

Now, he says, he finds himself at a similar crossroads. "I just need something that helps me explain more about today and where I am at," he says. "To explain some of these feelings that this world is going through right now, and trying to figure them out."

As LaFarge works to discover more of his authentic voice, he's quick to note that his journey of self-discovery is one with no known destination. "I don't know if I'll ever get to that point where I'll feel satisfied or say, 'This is my authentic self,' or even if I'll ever be happy," he says. "I don't think that's the point. I don't know if I can say I know anything else other than just writing, and finishing a record, and touring on it, at this point."

When pressed, he adds that he's not sure what the point of it all is – that sometimes he feels very small and insignificant, but that all he knows is to keep doing what he does in the best way possible.

"The feelings that I'm going through now," he says, "the ideas I'm having, I have to let them run their course and get the most out of this period." ■

We Are the Music Makers

BY TIM DUFFY

MUSIC MAKER RELIEF FOUNDATION

The blues, jazz, gospel, and old-time music of the American South forms a deep aquifer that contemporary musicians around the world drink from daily. The musicians portrayed here are the working-class fathers, mothers, and neighbors who continue to lovingly stir the South's musical stew and feed American culture. You probably won't recognize their names or faces, for few have found fame. Most of them weren't easy to find in the first place. But I traveled the South for 30 years, seeking the oldest guy that learned from the oldest guy who came before. And I founded the Music Maker Relief Foundation to provide assistance, build artists' careers, and nurture our musical heritage.

Joe Lee Cole
Bobo, Mississippi / 2001

Delta blues is filled with lore about its beginnings in toil and misery. For many artists, the hardships have still not been overcome. Joe Lee Cole lived outside Clarksdale, Mississippi, in a town called Bobo. His home was an old shack with one light bulb.

Benton Flippen
Mount Airy, North Carolina / 2006

Often heard on Mount Airy's WPAQ-AM since the 1940s,
Flippen's fiddle tunes are played by musicians worldwide.
He played for square dances every weekend in Surry
County, North Carolina, until his passing at the age
of 91. Benton would come to Music Maker's summer
picnics and just loved playing his bluesy fiddle – he
was the first to start playing and the last to stop.

Neal Pattman
Athens, Georgia / 1995

Neal loved his blues, singing and playing his
harp anywhere. He broke into a gospel song
every time he was about to take off on a plane.
Neal lost his arm in a farm accident at age
nine, but that didn't stop him from putting his
strength and size to use, running a drink house.

"Precious had a way of immediately pulling you into her soul. I'll never forget the first time I heard her. I knew I could never get enough of how she sang – her voice and the intimate wisdom with which she chose topics for her songs. Just so achingly perfect and, all at once, beautiful and personal!"

TAJ MAHAL

Precious Bryant & Lucas Duffy
Warm Springs, Georgia / 1995

Captain Luke (Luther B. Mayer)
Hillsborough, North Carolina / 2011

Captain Luke has a voice like honey dripping on hot
chocolate. Along with Guitar Gabriel, he was a king of
the Winston-Salem, North Carolina, drink house circuit.
When I first knocked on the doors of these unlicensed
bars in people's homes, they would be shut in my face.
Being young and white, folks assumed that I must
be the police. That was until Captain Luke took me
around for a year; after that, I was welcomed with
big smiles at all the local establishments.

Charly Lowry & Pura Fé Crescioni
Hillsborough, North Carolina / 2011

Pura Fé (*right*) challenges one's understanding of
Southern history as primarily a black and white story.
Her music highlights the intertwined lives and musical
traditions of African and native peoples. She notes, "Bred
together on plantations, the union gave birth to a rich
culture blending religion, dance, food, good-looking
people, and the blues." Pura Fé can trace native influences
on modern music from Charley Patton, who was
Choctaw, through Howlin' Wolf, to Elvis Presley.

"Blues is a legend,
it is something that will
be with us out through the
generations … You can go to
university, school, college,
but if you do not learn it in
the street, walking through
life, you will never really
learn it. That is what blues
is all about – it is a feeling.
You don't find it on notes
and paper. It comes
from the heart."

Guitar Gabriel
Lugano, Switzerland / 1992

George & Lula Daniels
Society Hill, Alabama / 2011

George is a bluesman with possibly the rankest electric guitar sound in the South. He is also a great singer and harmonica player, if you can get him to unplug his guitar. This photo was taken on a visit in 2011, when Music Maker discovered he had gone blind. He told us he was sitting around waiting for his sight to come back; he seemed completely certain that it would. He is still waiting.

Rufus McKenzie
Hillsborough, North Carolina / 1996

Rufus McKenzie sang in the ancient field holler
tradition. In "Slavery Time Blues," he sings of
getting a meal from a white woman while the
family dog growled in his direction:

I said Lady, I am sorry, I am sorry,
I believe your dog has seen a snake

She said no, no my friend,
you are eating from his plate

And you still want to know, why
the black man sings the blues?

DRAW ME IN, BLOW ME AWAY

How the humble harmonica became divine *by Kim Ruehl*

> ## "[With] a guitar, you can look down at the frets and see what you're playing. With harmonica, it just becomes part of your body."
>
> Mickey Raphael

TROSSINGEN IS A LONG WAY FROM the Mississippi Delta or the juke joints of Chicago, where so much of this story transpires. Situated in the hills of Southwest Germany, it's a stone's throw from Zurich and Lichtenstein, clear across the nation from the hipness and bustle of booming Berlin. And it's small – about nine square miles, filled with barely 16,000 people. But the story of Trossingen goes back centuries. Sure, there are the Plateosaurus bones found in a clay quarry on the edge of town. But for our purposes, the story starts getting interesting in the 1800s, in the workshop of a clockmaker named Christian Messner.

Toward the middle of that century, Messner and his cousin Christian Weiss started producing harmonicas in the downtime between clock jobs. Many believe they were building on the work of a fellow German named Christian Buschmann, who had the bright idea to produce a free reed pitch pipe in 1820. Unlike a saxophone, whose reed vibrates against a mouthpiece, or an oboe, whose sound is made by two reeds vibrating against one another, free reed instruments produce noise when a player blows air around a single reed, which in turn vibrates against the air. The length of the reed and the way it is

positioned determines what note results, so Buschmann's decision to create a pitch pipe through this method allowed tuners to be more exacting. Granted, he didn't create the notion of a free reed instrument. That credit is owed to the Chinese, who developed the first free reed gourd instrument, the sheng, somewhere around 1100 BC. But, by attaching a number of his pitch pipes together, Buschmann was among the first to use free reed technology to produce a Western scale. His creation, however, was such an awkward instrument that others fell in line to perfect it. The Messners produced the comb-and-plate structure that made the harmonica so accessible – 10 free reeds tuned along a single metal "plate," which is in turn mounted on a "comb," through which the player blows or draws. They cornered the Trossingen market for a few years before fellow clockmaker Matthias Hohner stopped by to see how they did it. Hohner saw a golden opportunity. He started making harmonicas in his shop, bought out the Messners, and mass-produced the instrument to market abroad.

As legend has it, Hohner sent a few of his harmonicas with cousins who were migrating to New York. They played them for friends, a trend caught on, and soon

Hohner harmonicas were being shipped over the Atlantic in great quantities. Such great quantities, in fact, that, by the turn of the century, the instrument could be purchased in any dime store for a nickel or so. By the 1920s, this little instrument based on ancient Chinese folk music, developed to produce German polka and oompah sounds, was proliferating throughout American cities and the rural South, where none of those musical vernaculars took root quite so deeply.

In the hands of Americans, the blow-and-draw method of music-making quickly led to new sounds. John Lee Williamson, who went by the stage name Sonny Boy, was the first harmonica star. While the story of the harmonica in Germany begins with Buschmann, Messner, and Hohner, its journey through American roots music, unequivocally, begins with Sonny Boy Williamson.

Sonny Boy's Blues Harp

Born in 1914 near Jackson, Tennessee, Williamson developed a blues harp playing style that came to characterize and motivate a generation of players. Most remarkable was his use of tone – a quality harmonica players, even in 2016, will name as the important thing to master with this instrument. Williamson's recordings depict an artist playing a very small number of notes. He'll stick on a single note or a triad run, playing it over and over. But the way his tone wraps around the notes, they change with every single blow. Somehow, with each repetition, the shape of the notes grows and evolves. The song pulls you somewhere, even if the melody isn't technically moving. You can't do that with any other instrument – except, perhaps, the human voice – with the same effect.

A giant of a man who went by the name of Howlin' Wolf would further Williamson's stripped-down playing.

In *Pocket Full of Soul: The Harmonica Documentary*, harp legend Charlie Musselwhite remembers Wolf. "Some guys, their tone is so good, they don't even need a few notes," he says. "A guy like Howlin' Wolf is like that. He only plays like five notes or something like that, but he could play just one note and – okay – that one note had everything. It was just this huge tone and when he hit that note, it was like, 'Wow! That's it.'"

Musselwhite is no mouse of a man himself. His harp playing is muscular and infectious. To watch him play, it looks like he is at once swallowing the instrument and spitting it out. He's not shy with the notes either. Where Wolf and Williamson stuck to the center of the harp, Musselwhite plays the way Aretha Franklin sings – tastefully, but with intangible power, with every note at his disposal. When I ask him about the relationship between singing and playing harmonica, he doesn't hesitate. "That's exactly it," he says. "It's just like singing without any words. I call it tunin'."

Musselwhite – who, at the beginning of his career, was given the name Memphis Charlie – was born in Mississippi but grew up in Memphis, Tennessee, stealing off into the woods with his harp for some alone time to master the thing. He landed in Chicago as a teenager, chasing a job outside of music, but it didn't take him long to find his way to the blues clubs. He spent so much time in those that the players on the circuit – Wolf, Muddy Waters, Junior Wells, Little Walter, and others – thought he was just their biggest fan. One night a waitress tipped off the band to the fact that this skinny little Native American kid could really play, and his life on the stage began. A half-century later, now living in San Francisco, Musselwhite has played with Bonnie Raitt and Ben Harper, Tom Waits and the Blind Boys of Alabama, and of course has made his own groundbreaking recordings. His career has helped shape the way the instrument is viewed by

mainstream music fans, but he's so humble on the phone, you'd think he was just coming up.

Of course, humility tends to be a common thread among harmonicists, a tight bunch to be sure. Every interview obtained for this article included a brief mention about who I'd already spoken with, followed inevitably by some variation of, "Oh, that guy's a good friend of mine." It's not surprising. This is a culture of musicians who have come to find glory on an instrument first marketed in the States as a toy. So deep was the perception of the harmonica's novelty during the early part of the 20th century, that one of the only American manufacturers of the instrument opted to make it entirely out of plastic. Its novelty was stretched further by its miniscule price tag – an instrument for poor folks and African-Americans, not for the "serious" musician or the concert stage.

During the 1930s, when there was a brief harmonica craze in the States that saw the rise of harp groups like Borrah Minevich's Harmonica Rascals and their offshoot troupe the Harmonicats, harmonicists were viewed as so much of a sideshow act, they weren't even allowed to join the musicians union. The Harmonicats were successful enough, however, that they hired a bassist and guitarist – accompaniment that lasted only until the union caught wind of it. Controversy followed, since it was uncouth for union players to play with what was disregarded as a joke act. Then the Harmonicats struck platinum with "Peg O' My Heart" – an instrumental B-side that sold one million copies in its first year. Guided by dollar signs, the union let them in.

The Rise of Walter and Butterfield

The Harmonicats' roaring mainstream success notwithstanding, the instrument was taking on a life of its own underground, at the same

Mickey Raphael's harmonica case.

> ## "Every harmonica player since Little Walter that plays the blues … is judged by how well they compare to Little Walter. Reason being, no other harmonica player had the soul, phrasing, and – most importantly in my book – time."
>
> Jason Ricci

time, particularly in Chicago. While you're likely to find some classical and jazz harmonicists these days who will sing the praises of Harmonicat Jerry Murad's tone, the influence of African-American players like Wolf, Williamson, James Cotton, and the game-changing magnificence of Little Walter had a far deeper and lasting effect on the entire umbrella of American roots music. This was partly due to those artists' influence on British rock bands, who didn't possess the same flavor of racial ignorance and bias that had been handed down to the white American youth of the period. Indeed, bands like the Beatles and the Rolling Stones – both fronted by harmonica players – were able to carry the influence of these Chicago cats into the ears of audiences who could not grasp how thoroughly harmonicists had contributed to the rise of these truly American musics. But, on whatever side of the pond one might train their retrospectoscope, the redefinition of the instrument and the kinds of music it could play during the Great Depression and early World War II era was largely in the hands of Chicago's Little Walter.

"Every harmonica player since Little Walter that plays the blues … is judged by how well they compare to Little Walter," says blues harpist Jason Ricci (Johnny Winter, Cedric Burnside) in *Pocket Full of Soul*. "Reason being, no other harmonica player had the soul, phrasing, and – most importantly in my book – time."

Indeed, Walter's harp playing blew the instrument into another dimension. The way he bent notes and turned phrases built atop the provenance of Williamson's legacy and provided a foundation for countless imitators. Walter's approach to the harp prevailed for decades, until Paul Butterfield upped the ante. Ricci's rant on the glory of Walter reaches its conclusion: "Nobody sounded like [Butterfield]," he enthuses. "You know, because *he* wasn't trying to sound like Little Walter."

In fact, aside from Butterfield's Blues Band's success in helping to catalyze Bob Dylan's rush from folk to rock music, the young harpist helped introduce the instrument – and the blues – to a generation of new players. Among them was a young musician in Dallas, Texas, named Mickey Raphael. In the '60s, Raphael was hanging out in the folk circuit, inspired by the music coming out of places like New York's Greenwich Village. He was a guitar player back then, and is the first to admit he was no good on that instrument. Then one night at a folk club, he saw blues harpist Donny Brooks onstage, his harmonica strutting through a melody with the kind of

swagger Brooks so masterfully played. Raphael knew right then that he had been barking up the wrong tree with the guitar. It didn't take him long to find his way to Butterfield.

"I'm not a straight player," Raphael says, decades later over the phone, musing about a Gershwin album he just recorded with his longtime bandmate Willie Nelson. "My strong point is my tone, and I've learned through the years that if you can play the melody, you really can't go wrong. Paul Butterfield taught me that. He said, 'Keep it simple.' He was my mentor."

Back in the 1960s, though, Raphael was hardly alone in his interest in the instrument. Baby boomers like himself had grown up with fathers who had received harmonicas as a gift from the United States government, to keep morale up as they were stationed overseas. Soldiers on both sides of World War II carried harmonicas in their pockets – an invisible line of common interest in one of the nastiest wars the world had seen. But as musicians back home got a hold of it, they discovered that, similar to the guitar or piano, the harmonica is a deceptively simple instrument to play; anyone can pick it up and blow a sound, but it is a considerably difficult instrument to play *well*.

Most Western instruments can be toyed about with by playing one note at a time. One can sit down at a piano and, with one finger, poke at the keys until they've fashioned out a melody. If one sticks only to the white keys, they've chosen to play either in the key of C Major or A Minor. They can see every note they play. Things only get complicated when they modulate to a different key or seek to add accompaniment, fill out chords and rhythms. The similar is true of any stringed instrument and all woodwinds and brass.

"[With] a guitar," Raphael explains, distilling the idea down to simplicity, the same way he plays his instrument, "you can look down at the frets and see what you're playing. With harmonica, it just becomes part of your body."

Charlie McCoy, whose career has seen him backing artists as variant as Roy Orbison, Elvis Presley, Johnny Cash, and Ween, explains further. "You only have ten holes on a harmonica," he says, "and [for] every one of them you have two choices: you can inhale or exhale. Harmonica is the only instrument that you can play both ways – inhale *and* exhale. Trumpet or saxophone, you can only play one way, and then you've got to breathe. But it's possible to play a whole song on the harmonica and never stop the notes."

In Touch with Your Soul

The fastest way to turn a harmonicist into a poet is to ask him or her about the relationship between the breath and the music. Though many musicians recognize a link between music and spirituality – whether it's the overtness of gospel music or the subtlety of taking in a Charlie Parker sax solo or a Mike Marshall mandolin run – the spiritual life force seems even more a driving factor in harmonica playing. Harmonicists' enthusiasm about what the breath is capable of echoes yogic philosophy in its intensity. "It's an instrument that's really in touch

with your soul," Raphael says, trying to explain what it is about the harmonica that gets so far under a player's skin – what part of it taps into the blues. "You breathe through this thing to make the sound, so it's really the closest thing to being a part of your body."

And, aside from the transformation of life-giving breath into life-sustaining music, harmonicists tend to have a relationship with their first harmonica that goes deeper than that of the players of most other instruments. This is likely because individual harmonicas don't last long. A guitarist can build a career from start to finish on the same guitar – ask Raphael's buddy Willie Nelson – but professional harmonicists need to tune or replace any one of their 12 harmonicas (one for each key) anywhere from every few weeks to every few months. No doubt, this places a special kind of sentimentality on the first one into which a player ever breathed.

Classical harmonicist Stan Harper found his first harp on the ground in New York City – something someone else discarded or lost. Raphael received his first harmonica as a gift from his dad's friend, who thought it'd make a nice little toy for him. Charlie McCoy, meanwhile, had to beg for his first instrument. "I started when I was eight years old," he says. "I saw it advertised in a comic book: 'You too can play harmonica in seven days, or your money back.' [It cost] 50 cents and a box top." He laughs. "Keep in mind this was 1949. Fifty cents was some money in 1949, especially to a single mom. I had to beg her for 50 cents.

"So," he continues, "I got a harmonica in the mail and I walked around the house making noise, and after a day she said, 'Could you take it outside?' But I realized, I found out I had a better than average ear and began to pick out some songs on it. I'm still picking out songs."

The size of a harmonica means picking one up and blowing into it results in some kind of automatic,

pre-programmed major and minor chord structure. Only the accordion similarly packs the instant gratification of feeling like you're one person creating an ensemble sound with a single musical movement. And that's no coincidence. The accordion and the harmonica come from the same family of instruments, and both have deep roots in German folk and classical music. But, where the accordion has been damned – at least until very recently – to the marginalized communities of polka and klezmer music, the harmonica crossed over into the mainstream nearly a century ago, beginning with Williamson's rise. The heavy influence of the Chicago players leapt into the mainstream when Bob Dylan stepped to the mic with one strapped into a rack, as some harp players would argue, for better or worse.

Long before and ever since, the instrument traveled the world in the pockets of countless others who never earned any kind of a living from their love for it. According to harmonicist Kim Field's exhaustive history, *Harmonicas, Harps, and Heavy Breathers: The Evolution of the People's Instrument*, five US presidents – Wilson, Coolidge, Eisenhower, Carter, and Reagan – were harmonica players. The instrument is a favorite of pop stars as different as Shakira and Clint Black. It's delivered concertos in the hands of maestro Larry Adler and twittering dances in the hands of John Popper. It's giggled and shuffled into the history books via diminutive Harmonica Rascal Johnny Puleo. Thanks to Williamson, Walter, and Butterfield, it changed the face of all styles of American music – blues, rock, pop, country, Americana, and even hip-hop, in the hands of Bad News Brown. And, considering its portability and implicit allure, it's easy to imagine that right now, somewhere in some woods, a child is breathing into a toy for the very first time, only to discover that thing is actually full of soul. ∎

"A guy like Howlin' Wolf ... he only plays like five notes or something like that, but he could play just one note and – okay – that one note had everything. It was just this huge tone and when he hit that note, it was like, 'Wow! That's it.'"

Charlie Musselwhite

FROM SIDEMAN TO THE MAN

Where Hubert Sumlin went with the blues
by Grant Britt

HE WAS THE MAN BEHIND THE MAN. That's what the general public thought, but musicians knew better. For anyone who played the blues, guitarist Hubert Sumlin was always *The Man*. His touch on the strings was unmistakable – a sound nobody else has been able to replicate, though a who's who of bluesmen have been trying to emulate it for decades.

By the time Sumlin passed away in 2011, his influence on the form was felt so heavily that Mick Jagger and Keith Richards covered the cost of his funeral. Shemekia Copeland sang a moving version of "Life's a Rainbow" at his graveside service. The following year, rock and blues royalty including Richards, Eric Clapton, Billy Gibbons, Elvis Costello, Jimmy Vaughan, Buddy Guy, Henry Gray, Eddie Shaw, and James Cotton came to pay their respects in song for 2012's Howlin' for Hubert at New York's Apollo Theatre.

Earlier in his career, overshadowed by Howlin' Wolf's larger-than-life persona, Sumlin was consigned to sideman status. But after Wolf passed,

Sumlin started to come into his own. Critics and musicians started to talk about what happened when his presence was detected on a tune, how his unique phrasing added a special mojo, a little extra something that was hard to describe but instantly recognizable as Sumlin's work the minute you heard it.

"Hubert's guitar playing was magical," says former Muddy Waters sideman Bob Margolin, who played and toured with Sumlin in his later years. "Endlessly creative, and I could not figure out how he did it by watching his fingers, which seemed to dance gracefully over his guitar neck. He created the tone and signature licks with his fingers, had a trademark sound on any guitar he used. I have heard many guitar players be inspired by him, but none that sounded like him."

It Started with One String

Born in 1931 in Greenwood, Mississippi, Sumlin learned to play by experimenting with a diddley bow – a one-stringed creation his brother had rigged up, attached to the side of their sharecropper shack. But his first attempt at using the contraption ended in disaster: Sumlin's older brother claimed Hubert broke the instrument and sought retribution.

"I didn't break the string, 'cause how can you break baling wire? You bale hay with it," Sumlin told me in a 2007 interview. The guitarist was battling lung cancer by then, and the complications from that fight would take him four years later. But even though he had lost a lung at that point in his career and had to perform sitting down, he never lost his eagerness to perform. He was gracious and funny, always humble, and enjoyed making new friends wherever he traveled. You could talk to him for five minutes and he'd make you feel like you'd been friends for life.

"What happened was," Sumlin continued, "I slid that bottle down that one string and it came unwound around the nail. And so my brother says I broke it. Man, he got mad, boy. He's a big ol' boy. And he hit me. He slapped me, man, and Lord, I saw stars and everything."

But Sumlin's mother took his side, telling him she was going to lay a whupping on the older boy. "When we got to the house, he was gone," Sumlin chuckled. "He didn't come back for three days. He knowed what was gonna happen to him."

For those three days, Sumlin had the instrument to himself, and he was determined to become proficient on it. His brother, once he returned, added more strings to the diddley bow until there were four. Sumlin's skills on those strings impressed his mother so much she bought him a real guitar.

"I learned how to play it," he said. "Then for three weeks I didn't let my brother play on that guitar at all. Every day I'd get that guitar and at night, too, man, and sit around the house and on the porch and play, and he would be right there. He didn't go nowhere. He didn't eat right." Sumlin cackled. "I felt sorry for him, so I gave him the guitar. And he started to play, one finger, like he did on the side of the wall. But he learned how to play better than me. He was my influence on guitar."

Hired and Fired

Sumlin left home in his early teens, teaming up with James Cotton. He and Cotton cut a single, "Cotton Crop Blues," that Wolf heard and liked so much he gave Cotton and Sumlin 15 minutes of his 30-minute radio show on KWEM in West Memphis, Arkansas.

"We got so good with that 15 minutes he gave us, he taken his 15 minutes back," Sumlin recalled. "But he said 'Hubert, I'm going to Chicago. I'm gonna get you.'"

In 1953, Wolf asked Sumlin to join him. "I looked at Cotton and he said, 'Man, you go on with Wolf, you'll make more money with him than you will with me.'"

The partnership Sumlin formed with Howlin' Wolf lasted for over 20 years. Sumlin became an arranger as well as a sideman. "He would ask me how the music go," the guitarist remembered. "That's right – *any* music."

Even classic Wolf tunes like "Built for Comfort" benefitted from Sumlin's adaptations. "We got to playing it over and over again, so I started thinking I'm gonna change the way we first recorded it," Sumlin said. "And so what I did, I find out his voice – on all his numbers you got to at least be saying something, you got to have your tone of voice."

Sumlin says the two communicated so well that he knew what Wolf was going to do musically before he did it. "In other words, we were communing together," he says. "I *knowed* the guy, man."

But as innovative as Sumlin was, Wolf felt he could do better. So, in the middle of a gig, he gave his guitarist a motivational boost that didn't seem like much of a blessing at the time. Wolf fired Sumlin in front of 700 people. "Oh man, I could have killed him," Sumlin says. "I got so mad. Lord, man, I ain't never felt so bad in all my days."

The band was in the middle of "Smokestack Lightnin'," and Wolf apparently felt Sumlin was adding too many notes to the mix. "I saw him turn a color, I knowed what that meant, man," Sumlin said. "I knowed he was mad. And he said, 'You been playing with me all these years, man. And you so fast with that straight pick. Just go home and put your pick down. And try your fingers.' And he called somebody out of the audience to take my place."

Heartbroken and humiliated, Sumlin went home, dried his tears, and started to work on his fingerpicking.

"I put that pick down and went to playing with my fingers, man, and all my fingers got sore, got so sore."

But Sumlin eventually found salvation on the same tune that had damned him. "I got 'Smokestack Lightnin',"' he said, looking back. "I found my own self, I found my own tune, my own sound. I had what he needed." He chuckled. "I had the music, and he had the voice."

Wolf took him back, and the duo remained together until Wolf's death in 1976. But even though Sumlin thought of Wolf as a father figure, the relationship was rocky. Sumlin said he was fired and rehired sometimes in as little as five minutes, and he recalled one time both men performed impromptu dentistry on each other.

"He knocked my teeth out and I knocked his out," Sumlin told the *Milwaukee Journal Sentinel* in a 1998 interview. "I got three or four punches in first. You didn't want him to land on top of you," he said of the 300-pound Wolf. "He was something, man. The day after the fight he went and had the teeth fixed with gold. He looked better than before I hit him."

"I found my own self, I found my own tune, my own sound. I had what [Howlin' Wolf] needed. I had the music, and he had the voice."

Hubert Sumlin

Despite the dust-ups, Wolf remained intensely loyal to Sumlin. Muddy Waters wanted Sumlin for his band, and at one point hired him away from Wolf after one of their conflagrations. Sumlin got fed up with the arrangement after he had driven nonstop from Miami to Chicago for a gig because everybody else in Waters' band was drunk. So he called Wolf, and Wolf came in and told Muddy, "I come to get my son. But you know what? Muddy, I ain't gonna do you like you did me. You can have this guitar player I got. I ain't gonna leave you stranded.'"

Sumlin chuckled at the memory. "And Muddy started cryin', man. [He said,] 'Oh man, I don't like this.'" Waters pointed at Sumlin and said through his tears, "'This guy know all I know. I don't have to play.' And Wolf said, 'Oh yes you do. You do now.'"

Waters wasn't the only musician who recognized Sumlin's unique contribution. When Wolf was summoned to London to record the Chess Records *Howlin' Wolf Sessions* with the Rolling Stones and Eric Clapton, Sumlin wasn't included.

"The Chess Brothers told Wolf they didn't want me to go," says Sumlin, "because the Rolling Stones, they were trying to mate with Wolf, ... were trying to get on his record. And they figured out that if I was a little bit hindered, if I wasn't playing [with Wolf], they were gonna [get to] play what I was going to play. But I knew better. I *knowed* Wolf – they was gonna play what he played, what he wanted 'em to play."

Then, while plans were still being made, Leonard Chess got a call from Clapton. "Clapton says 'Hey, I know what happened.' ... He said to old Chess, Leonard, if [Sumlin] didn't come and be

on this set with him, [then Clapton] wasn't coming. Oh yeah."

Sumlin got his plane ticket, played on the album, and walked away with a lifetime friendship with Clapton.

Always Ready to Go

Sumlin's talent and personality impressed everyone who came in contact with him. Greensboro, North Carolina-based bassist Bobby Kelly toured and roomed with Sumlin in 2008 on several dates led by Bob Margolin. "A sweeter, more gentle man I've never met in my life," Kelly says. "You're always cautious about meeting your heroes, because more often than not, your view of them becomes soiled. I've never met a guy that had more of a song in his heart at all times."

Kelly remembers Sumlin sitting next to him in the van, quietly singing licks and songs to himself. "Music just oozed out of this guy. He was always ready to go. And he knew what a gift he had been given."

Kelly says that gift was apparent on the London Howlin' Wolf sessions, when Sumlin led the Stones and Clapton from behind. "Those guys studied him as kids growing up, so when they finally got a chance to play with him, you hear him still teaching these guys how to play this stuff."

"If you listen carefully to that record, you'll hear Hubert doing what Wolf was asking him to do and asking the other guys to do," Kelly says. "And Hubert, without saying a word, showing them by example what to play. It's such an amazing lesson, so deep on so many levels."

Kelly views what Sumlin was doing as the blues equivalent to what Funk Brothers bassist James Jamerson did on the Motown sessions. "You take the bass

parts out of that catalog and you ain't got shit. With all due respect, there were wonderful other people who played on that stuff. But that was the spark plug that made all the rest of it work, and Hubert was that guy."

Like Margolin, Kelly watched Sumlin's hands while he performed, but says that even an up-close look at what he was doing was hard to put into words. "He could just take a basic groove and put a signature lick on it – this icing-on-the-cake thing that was just perfect," Kelly says. "It's not about playing a lot of notes; it's about playing the right notes, dodging and weaving but still making it real lyrical, making it undeniably Hubert Sumlin."

Even though Sumlin was confident of his abilities, Wolf's death in '76 so devastated him that he wouldn't play for months afterward and thought about retiring altogether. Gradually, he returned to recording and touring, and moved from Chicago to Milwaukee, Wisconsin, in 1989. He enlisted Keith Richards to play on his 2004 solo album, *About Them Shoes*. Despite failing health, he played festivals and clubs until his death.

But perhaps the best summation of his life and work is taken from Sumlin's own words in my last interview with him. After we'd talked for about 20 minutes, Sumlin decided he was through talking and was ready to prove he could still bring it. But befitting his humble nature, he chose not to strut, allowing his talent to speak for itself.

"I tell you what," he said, chuckling in anticipation of getting out in front of an audience who revered him as *The Man*, not just the sideman. "When I get there, man, I'm gonna do my best." ∎

ROCK ME

The lasting legacy of Sister Rosetta Tharpe

by Erin Lyndal Martin

> "Her example of self-sufficiency stands out, a kind of career that had ups and downs but wasn't defined by a Svengali-like man or by her decline into victimization. So she stands out as this interesting example of a woman who tried to have a career on her own terms as long as she could."
>
> Gayle Wald

THERE ARE MANY WAYS TO TELL the story of Sister Rosetta Tharpe, but all angles converge on one thing: her work ethic. Combined with her showmanship and remarkable talent, it earned her a long dynamic career. In videos of her performances, Tharpe wears her trademark evening gown and flirts coquettishly with the audience. You can get wrapped in her personality, but then her voice rings out full, round tones glorifying God, even as she grabs her guitar to shake and shimmy as if in spirit possession.

Then there's her legacy, which there's no denying. Johnny Cash said she was his favorite musician. Keith Richards looks up to her guitar prowess, and she had a deep influence on Elvis Presley. Tharpe's tours to the UK made her a source of inspiration for the British Invasion. And today, still, numerous musicians who span the gamut of genre, race, and gender consider her a great inspiration – not just musically, but also as a performer, and as someone strategic enough to overcome all the obstacles and limits she faced, so long as she could keep making music.

Moving the Audience

Rosie Etta was born to Katie Harper and Willis Atkins in Cotton Plant, Arkansas, in early 1915. (Tharpe was her first husband's last name.) She grew up in the Church of God in Christ – a small, then relatively new branch of the Pentecostal Church. Thus, to tell the story of Sister Rosetta Tharpe, one must also tell the story of COGIC.

The church's strict rules governed women's appearance: they could not wear makeup or jewelry and were not permitted to either lighten or darken their skin or hair. Yet, contrary to these rules that aimed to steer congregants away from vanity, there was a rich emotional expressiveness to the church. Revivals were chaotic and could go on for hours, congregants and preachers intuiting when to interrupt one another with a song or a sermon.

"The Church of God in Christ ... is a Pentecostal denomination that was already open to, first of all, praising God with instruments, but also praising God with all kinds of instruments – including those that were not looked upon fondly in other more mainline churches, like Baptist churches or Methodist churches," says Tharpe biographer Gayle Wald, author of *Shout Sister Shout*. "So she grew up in a church context where horns were welcome, drums were welcome, acoustic guitars were welcome. I think it was the liberalism of the church around what the music of worship could sound like that really shaped her musical sensibility. ... [Those] church audiences already knew that and weren't as interested in music just for pleasure, or music as a way of moving the body, certainly – moving the body in a way that wasn't about giving glory to God."

Here among the dichotomy of restrictions and bombastic expression, Sister Rosetta Tharpe spent her early years shaping into the star she'd become. More than happy to toss aside rules about appearances (at the end of her life, she had an entire shed devoted to storing her gowns), Tharpe kept that flamboyant spirit alive throughout her career.

Still, as restrictive as COGIC was, it may have offered Tharpe an agency of musical expression that was harder to find in the music business. "Commercial music didn't necessarily give her agency as a female performer," Wald explains. "In some ways, I think the church had afforded her more agency and authority as a female performer. Those first records for Decca, where she's accompanying herself, she doesn't need to be anyone's frontwoman; she's a kind of self-sufficient soloist. They become powerful evidence that, even what seems like a socially and sexually restrictive environment for women – like the Pentecostal church, where you're not allowed to wear makeup and you're not allowed to date and you're not allowed to dance and you're

not allowed to have any sexuality – paradoxically, that could be a space where she had musical and cultural authority. As opposed to when she went with [bandleader Lucky] Millinder in the secular realm, she had apparently more access to being a sexual object, but it was at the cost of being constructed as an object of the male gaze. And also, she didn't get to play her instrument the same way. ... There were attempts to give her the stage, but that wasn't her only or primary goal."

Indeed, Tharpe first came to fame as the frontwoman for Lucky Millinder's swing band. Later, she and vocalist Marie Knight developed a long-term musical, friendly, and romantic relationship. Knight, with her pretty contralto, proved to be an excellent complement to Tharpe's own voice, and the two had chemistry – fluidly trading off on vocals, featuring Tharpe turning toward the piano instead of the wild applause. Together, they produced hits like the spirited "Up above My Head," which Rhiannon Giddens revived for her 2015 album *Tomorrow Is My Turn*.

That said, while it would be easy to point to restrictions Tharpe faced from record labels, from a racially segregated society, and from a couple awful marriages, this is not a story about how a great musician found limitations and restrictions and oppression at every turn. Instead, it's a story about how she always had a strategy up her sequined sleeve, a way to move through her career with a resilient jubilation.

Despite all the things that could have kept her down, Sister Rosetta Tharpe found her strength in rising above oppression. It is harder to say whether that transcendence or her musical and performance prowess has contributed more to her legacy. But what we do know is that Tharpe has been inspiring musicians for decades, and those musicians pass her name to others.

Light into Darkness

Singer Joan Osborne, whose voice balances clear soul and gospel influences, remembers her early encounters with Tharpe's music. "I was very interested in the fact that she was a big star in her era and she came out of gospel music but not in typical gospel settings," she says. "She became this huge sensation because she was mixing those two worlds and it was very controversial at the time. But it seemed like her philosophy was, 'This music needs to be in places where there's darkness,' which she considered the nightclub world to be – the light that she was bringing was necessary. So I was impressed by the fact that she was able to stand in both places. You don't get to do that unless you are incredibly talented and gifted enough to entertain people and get your message across. You have to have both of those abilities, and she certainly had them.

"She had a huge amount of charisma," Osborne adds. "She was an excellent guitar player, very influential in her guitar playing. ... I also love a lot of the material she did. That song 'Strange Things Happen Every Day,' that's such a great hook to talk about the mysterious things that happen in our lives. She would attribute them to spiritual causes and faiths and beliefs, but you could also take this broader perspective of the mysteries of life, or a religious lens or a spiritual lens or a broader, almost Buddhist take on it. As a songwriter, there are certain things in her lyrics that ring out to me, that have this really cool sort of frisson, that suggest this deeper reality that all of us are connected to."

Singer-songwriter Toshi Reagon's mother, Bernice, was a Student Nonviolent Coordinating Committee Freedom Singer and founder of Sweet Honey in the Rock. The elder Reagon built her career straddling the line between gospel music and socially conscious songs, and it was through her that Toshi discovered Tharpe. "My mom,"

L to R: Lucky Millinder, Sister Rosetta Tharpe, and Tharpe's agent Moe Gale.

"There are certain things in her lyrics that ring out to me, that have this really cool sort of frisson, that suggest this deeper reality that all of us are connected to."

Joan Osborne

Toshi Reagon says, "she did a version of 'Precious Memories' with Sweet Honey in the Rock. But she talked about her before because she played guitar and sang, and I played guitar and sang when I was young. So I was always looking for women guitar players to be like, 'Well, see, I come from a line!' It was great for my mother to introduce me to her because she had started so early and she was way before a lot of guitar players, male or female, that I liked. It was a great gift that my mother gave me, that I was in the right place [for], because of her."

Like Reagon, folksinger Janis Ian remembers her thirst for female guitarist role models. "She and Victoria Spivey – along with Nina Simone – were pretty much the only female players and band leaders I was aware of as I came up," Ian says. "Sister Rosetta played guitar like the men I was listening to, only smoother, with bigger notes – if that makes any sense. And of course, personally, *any* female player was a big influence on me, because there were so few."

Ian is right that, then and now, women are less likely to receive accolades for their guitar playing, more likely to be heralded for "playing as good as the guys." Thus, Sister Rosetta Tharpe seems like an anomaly now, considering

how many worlds she inhabited, but she was also an anomaly among her contemporaries.

Companions and Curiosity

Nonetheless, she was not the only woman who was known for playing guitar in the first part of the 20th century. Memphis Minnie (also known as Lizzie "Kid" Douglas), who taught herself banjo and guitar as a child, was one of a few notable female guitarists/singer-songwriters. But Memphis Minnie's music and life followed a different path than Sister Rosetta Tharpe's. Minnie toured with the Ringling Brothers Circus for a few years, then returned to live among the blues on Beale Street. There, she supplemented the income from her music with prostitution, which was not uncommon for performers at that time.

Tharpe's gospel peers also stood apart from her. Though she was most often juxtaposed with the gospel singer Mahalia Jackson, that comparison isn't exactly parallel. Jackson avoided secular crowds and flashy clothes, and she didn't play guitar. But the frequency with which they were compared says more about the media's need to pit two black female gospel musicians against each other than it does any similarities in their approach to the music.

In fact, aside from both having worked in the gospel idiom, Tharpe and Jackson could not be more different. Master guitarist and singer-songwriter Bonnie Raitt agrees. "Rosetta was a pioneer in several fields," she says. "She was the first black gospel artist to appear at the Apollo Theater [in 1943]. She had a major label recording contract with Decca that spanned three decades. She hosted her own syndicated gospel television program from 1962 to '64. She was one of the few women lead guitar players at that time; Memphis Minnie was the only other one of any prominence. Unlike her contemporary, Mahalia Jackson, who stood tall and strong and very still onstage when she sang gospel, Rosetta Tharpe was an *entertainer* – her sprightly stage presence contrasted well with the spiritual content of her songs."

That sprightly stage presence had a lot to do with Tharpe's fame and following, especially among white listeners. For them to see that gospel could swing, that an African-American woman in a swanky dress could be upbeat – even in songs petitioning God for help – was new and, notably, nonthreatening. Her songs generally weren't political and didn't directly address race issues – topics that had often put white audiences off of listening to black singers. Plus, she was beyond charming, belting out her songs while she played guitar so hard that the instrument seemed more like a dance partner than an electrified piece of wood.

Nonetheless, in her day, African-American women who became famous musicians, especially those with instruments, initially were regarded as a novelty. Wald tells of one notable performance by Tharpe at Carnegie Hall, at an event dubbed "From Spirituals to Swing" – a landmark 1938 concert of black music performed for an integrated audience. When Tharpe performed, Wald says, "she was situated more as a kind of ethnographic curiosity for audiences. I don't mean to say that there was no appreciation of her music, but where she was onstage is a wonderful example of the music being produced in black churches."

"The audience for From Spirituals to Swing," she adds, "which would have been a culturally elite audience, white audience in 1938, would have received her with a kind of enthusiastic curiosity. She was kind of a spectacle. Musically or culturally, swing was there, but also the folkloric discovery of the 'American South' and its traditions, and the *black* American south – I think that shaped her reception, at least among white audiences.

"As far as I could tell when I was doing research for the book," she continues, "she had a wide range of audiences. She appealed to white Southerners and black Southerners. She had exposure to fans of commercial swing music through Lucky Millinder. The church would have known about her and responded to her. There [were] people listening to country music who knew about her. And generations of rock and rollers in the United States and Britain that discovered her at some point. So she had this broad audience."

Both Sides of the Line

In part, Tharpe's audience was so broad because the work she did was broad.

While a lot of gospel-bred musicians abandoned sacred music for blues or the burgeoning sounds of rock and roll, Tharpe never lost her gospel edge, even when she was rocking out in nightclubs. "But she's really complicated because she tried to straddle the line between sacred and secular," explains Wald. "That made her a controversial figure and an attractive figure, and that challenges some of our ways of understanding that line between the two – understanding that there is a line between the two. Al Green goes back and forth, but she was someone who stayed committed to the church her whole career, but also brought that church music to a secular audience. So I think that that makes her really interesting and potentially different from other musicians who followed a similar path."

Despite the success her sound brought her, Tharpe carried sorrow over being ostracized from certain church populations because her music swung and she performed in nightclubs. "I've certainly heard rumblings that she wanted to go back to church music because her music was controversial in a lot of conservative church circles," says Osborne. "She didn't want that rejection from those people; she felt like she wanted to go back and do straighter gospel music. But because this style had been more successful for her, she was really pushed away from that. … It's not something I have a great knowledge of, [but] I think what she was able to do in that moment – whether she wanted to or not – was to really expand an audience for gospel music. Maybe that was the personal price that she had to pay in being ostracized by members of her community.

"If you can look at it from the [distance] that we can look at it from in this day and age," she adds, "you really can see that what she was doing, a lot of people who came after her did as well. They took gospel and expanded the audience. Somebody like Mavis Staples and the Staple Singers, somebody like Sam Cooke – they were following in those footsteps as well. It seems like it had this air of inevitability about it because the music is so powerful you can't keep it sequestered in this tiny community. It's something that can travel to a lot of places, and will."

Tharpe's breakthrough hit, "Rock Me," is a perfect example of how she blurred the line between gospel and rock. The lyrics, adapted from lines penned by Tommy Dorsey, are ambiguous enough that she could be talking about either a lover or Jesus:

You hold me in the bosom
Til the storms of life are over
Rock me in the cradle of your love

Her impassioned vocals encompass both a pleading tone and a praising one. "Rock Me" is a song that captures Tharpe so perfectly, with one foot in the sacred world and the other in the secular.

On an album made to pay tribute to Tharpe, *Shout Sister Shout*, which was curated by drummer and producer Mark Carpentieri, Toshi Reagon gave her interpretation of the song. Since Reagon wasn't provided with a lyric sheet, she guessed at the words after hearing the recording, which led her to sing "Tie me" instead of "Hide me" in one of the verses on the album. But for Reagon, that mistake just added to the mythos. "Now that I understand a lot of the context of her recording that song," she says, "I actually don't mind my lyric [mistake]. I like that song because it says 'rock me,' and it says 'rock me in the cradle of your love until the storm is over.' That really shaped my arrangement, and I like anything that asks to be heard. It's a song that's very much like, *Hear me*. Later, when I found out it was part of her transition into the secular world, I thought that was probably a song she was trying to ground herself in as she was doing something that was very new for her."

Reagon says she knew right away that her arrangement would be funky, and she wanted a contemporary gospel vocal on the chorus. The bridge, too, has a gospel influence, but Reagon wanted to highlight a guitar in honor of Tharpe's own instrument. Asked about the sensuality in her version, Reagon laughs. "People have said they thought there was so much sensuality in my version, and it's so funny because I was not thinking about that at all. I was thinking straight-up spiritual and call to the universe, to

hide me and protect me and help me get through things that are too hard for me. And other people were listening to it saying, 'It's so sensual,' and I was just like, 'Y'all are crazy! You're looking for sex in everything.' Just cause it has a wah-wah guitar in it doesn't mean I'm trying to fuck somebody.

"In a lot of sacred music, the sacred has to do with everything," she explains. "It doesn't just have to do with this little corner in your heart that belongs to Jesus or belongs to Buddha or whoever you pray to. It doesn't have to do with that tiny little place. It has to do with your entire being."

Married to the Job

Tharpe would almost certainly have agreed with Reagon, given her knack for blending the churchy with the pure fun. No event encapsulates this better than Tharpe's wedding – her third – to Russell Morrison in 1951.

The event was planned as a big wedding/concert at Griffith Stadium in Washington, DC, and Tharpe was to be the bride. These things were planned with only one thing missing: a groom. The search began for one, and, in the end, Morrison was chosen. The nuptials were quick and then the concert commenced, complete with Tharpe, still in her wedding dress, playing in the outfield. Church groups, music fans, and a diverse array of others attended the festivities. The crowd was said to number 25,000 people.

Music critic Greil Marcus referred to the wedding as "a classic American tall tale, except that it happened." In an article for the magazine *CounterPunch*, Scott Borchert writes, "Looking back, the wedding seems like a crude publicity stunt, and in many respects, it was. But isn't there another way to see it? Imagine Sister Rosetta in the midst of that absurd scene, her wedding gown billowing, with fireworks blazing overhead and her amplifier ringing. 'Get a load of this,'

she might be thinking. 'What a farce! But at least we'll get an LP out of it – and a great concert!'

"The wedding was a means to an end," he continues, "but the end was not Russell Morrison or a vow to any man. The vow was to her music, and the groom, in a sense, was incidental. It's as though the ceremony was a declaration that Sister Rosetta would be wedded first and foremost to her musical career – to her fans, perhaps, and to herself – and that nothing else deserved her full and total devotion. For this act alone – ridiculous and defiant and inspiring all at once – she ought to be remembered."

And that image – Tharpe resounding from the outfield with that perpetual smile on her face – is what has lasted, indeed. It's an iconic moment, summing up so much of what made her so powerful.

Trying to tease out some of what made Sister Rosetta Tharpe so unique, Wald says, "She had a kind of energy that was partly energy she had modeled after the Pentecostal church she came from. But she had an energy to connect with her audience. She did that as a vocalist but also as a guitarist. And she was also a kind of very spectacular performer with regards to her guitar. And early with the electric guitar in the '40s, but even before that when she was still playing an acoustic instrument, she figured out – there's not a word for showmanship that has to do with women but I think she figured out how to make the guitar an aspect of her onstage show. Watching her with her daredevil moves was pretty spectacular and got people excited."

It's natural but unfortunate that many people praise Tharpe simply by talking about those she influenced. While her work did inspire a lot of early rock and roll greats, Tharpe deserves her due for being her own musician. The fact that this so rarely happens is no doubt due in part to her novelty as a talented female guitarist. But there's also the problem of white musicians who

> **" She was a great show-woman. She was a great guitarist. She was a great vocalist. … She could play with a small band, she could play with a giant choir, she could do anything."**
>
> Toshi Reagon

appropriate the music and performance style of musicians of color and then receive more accolades.

"But if you see how people contextualize her," Reagon says, "they contextualize her against what white people think is great. White people say 'She influenced Elvis! Look!' And I'm, like 'Fuck Elvis, man. Come on, did that man not get enough?' [Or,] 'She was the godmother of rock and roll!' [I think,] 'Fuck rock and roll!' [But] that is white people's bar for us. They never want to see that she was over Elvis. At the end of the day, Elvis was a cool white guy who could sing some black music okay. He was a great showman. He sold a million records. But if y'all had not oppressed every black person up to that point, he would not be able to stand.

"The context to [Sister Rosetta's] greatness," Reagon continues, "is based on white oppression of black artists. And it's insanity. No, you can't hold her up to Elvis. Elvis is Elvis because you would never give somebody else on the same platform who was a black person – that he was copying – the same exact space that you gave him. You never would. Elvis cannot be the context for Sister Rosetta Tharpe. And rock and roll cannot be the context for Sister Rosetta Tharpe. She was bigger than both, and using those lines to try to say 'that's what she was' is people trying to give other people a teaching guide."

So, while Tharpe's work may often be seen in a context that slights her, it's undeniable that she's influenced others both through her music and her life. Wald talks about some of those influences both in the US and in Europe: "She's influenced directly a large number of female musicians – not just guitarists but her example of self-sufficiency stands out, a kind of career that had ups and downs but wasn't defined by a Svengali-like man or by her decline into victimization. So she stands out as this interesting example of a woman who tried to have a career on her own terms as long as she could. And she was really adept at her instrument.

"For a lot of women musicians," she adds, "that ends up being a really inspiring example. There was a whole generation of young people who were exposed to her in Europe in the late '50s through the late '60s, so for about a decade. And that generation would be part of the generation that would constitute the British Invasion, so there's these layers of influence she has. She was probably the most well-known American woman touring in the '50s and '60s with these, they called them gospel caravans or blues caravans, that were organized. So she had a more contemporary influence in Europe at a time when the US audience was fading."

An Endless Well

Unfortunately, Tharpe's career was cut short by her illness and death in 1973, but she lived every moment of it. After one of her legs had to be amputated, she still performed – sometimes hopping around the stage on one leg. She *had* to make music and she had to perform it, and maybe that's the simplest way to describe her career.

"She was a great show-woman," says Reagon. "She was a great guitarist. She was a great vocalist. She was a great interpreter of texts. She had the most fierce enunciation of anybody. She had excellent phrasing. She could play with a small band, she could play with a giant choir, she could do anything."

"She's part of the canon of artists who you're able to go back again and again to that well for inspiration," Osborne adds. "And you may not have listened for five or six years, but you listen again and you hear some other shade of meaning in the words or connect with some other aspect of what she's doing rhythmically, or with the guitar. [Her music is] just a source, it's a well you go back to again and again. I'm sure that there are many people besides me who look to her for that kind of inspiration."

And they will keep on looking, especially as Tharpe's name becomes more known to a new generation. In 2009, she finally received a proper headstone after years of lying in an unmarked grave in Philadelphia. Writer and publisher Bob Merz heard an interview with Gayle Wald and was moved to organize a concert to raise money for the stone. Tharpe's friend Roxie Moore wrote the epitaph: "She would sing until you cried and then she would sing until you danced for joy. She helped to keep the church alive and the saints rejoicing." A fitting tribute, but we all know Sister Rosetta Tharpe is still singing. ∎

SOUL-FULL

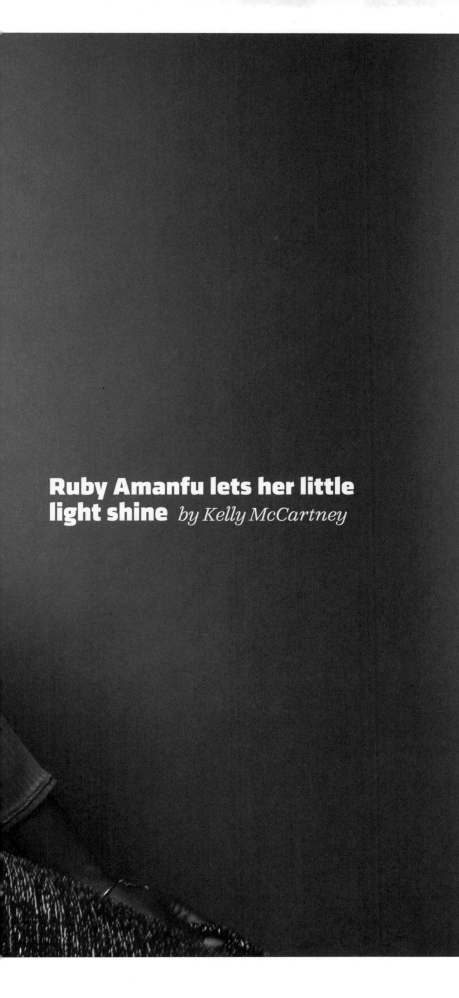

Ruby Amanfu lets her little light shine *by Kelly McCartney*

EVERY NOW AND THEN, AN ARTIST comes along who is at once transcendent and humble, and in one listen, you know Ruby Amanfu is such an artist. She moves her audience's emotions alongside her own as she winds her way through a song. It's an intangible gift she brings to bear, and one that she discovered at a very young age.

Born in Accra, Ghana, Amanfu and her family moved to Nashville, Tennessee, when she was three years old. Her family was both musical and religious, so she got her start singing in church. "I always get a chuckle on the inside when I say that quote, 'I started singing in the church,'" she says, "because I grew up in very classically contemporary Christian music. That's where it was at.

"Contemporary Christian music is very much 'Let's modernize a sound to reach more people' ... so I was singing a lot of vanilla songs," she adds. "Later, we moved to a church that did start adding true gospel music in there, music with energy. That was definitely more fun when you could clap on the 2 and 4, and move to the beat. Everyone was dancing in the rows, just flailing."

At home, the classical and Christian influences persisted, with Amanfu's musical tastes being guided by her father's, and those voices continue to shape who she is as an artist.

The Spirit Coming Through

When asked, Amanfu rattles off the artists that loom large for her. "Mavis [Staples] would be in there," she says, "because she's somebody my dad listened to. I think a big one is also Shirley Caesar. She is a powerhouse gospel singer. If we're going to go back, I would also say Kathleen Battle is a big one. Dianne Reeves, Sarah Vaughn, Bill Withers ... " Her voice trails off, but it would seem fitting to find Sweet Honey in the Rock in there, too. To that, her voice rises in enthusiastic agreement, "They came to my college once and I was like, 'Are you kidding me?!' I cried the whole time.

"[But] Kathleen Battle and Jessye Norman," she adds, "even though these are classical singers, you hear them sing a spiritual and it sounds soul-filled and soul-full."

Songwriter Bonnie Baker – who has penned tunes for Rachel Platten and Striking Matches and has known Amanfu for more than a decade – hears that same spirit coming through her. "One voice I hear in Ruby is Nina Simone's," she says. "It's not the sound, exactly; it is more the texture of her soul that oozes out of every pore of her being when she sings. That is the way Nina Simone always brought her music to her audience. Ruby is one of those artists that make you *experience* her music versus just *listening* to it. [Ruby's] soul is deep and dark, peaceful and chaotic, beautiful and broken, healing and rich ... and pure light."

Meanwhile, outside of church, Amanfu stepped into various talent shows and began to find her voice as both a singer and a songwriter. She attended Nashville's acclaimed Hume-Fogg Academic Magnet High School, where she participated in the fine arts program and recorded original songs in the school's studio. When she was 15, she was tapped to join the Nashville Symphony Chorus – its youngest-ever member. As a junior, she wrote, recorded, and co-produced her debut album, *So Now*

the Whole World Knows. The effort showed enough talent to earn her entry to Berklee College of Music in Boston. She eventually transferred to Belmont University back in Nashville, landed a record deal, and worked with Grammy-nominated producer/songwriter Tommy Sims on a song called "Sugah" that anchored her *Smoke & Honey* album in 2003.

Even as all of that solo work was happening, Amanfu was collaborating with singer-songwriter Sam Brooker on the side. The two had met in 1999 at a writer's round, finding a personal friendship first and, within a few years, an artistic kinship as well. "Ruby and I started off as friends," Brooker says. "I don't even think she told me she did music, initially. Then, she had a show and I went. ... She was mesmerizing on stage. It was like I was looking at a superstar.

"It took us a long time to even talk about music together," he adds. "It was three years later, after me wet, that we decided to write a song. That first song we ever wrote, 'The Here and the Now' – she'd gotten a lead that T Bone Burnett was looking for songs for the *Ya-Ya Sisterhood* movie, so she called me up and said, 'Let's write a song for it.'"

The song didn't make the film, but as Sam & Ruby, the pair easily found fans. Their eponymous, independent EP in 2006 created such a stir that the 2009 Rykodisc release of *The Here and the Now* landed a top spot on the Associated Press's "Best Albums" list. Brooker cites Amanfu's part in the magic. "I think Ruby has a difference in the way she thinks about music, from a melody standpoint," he says. "She writes more poetically. There's songwriting and then there's poetry, and I think Ruby is somewhere in the middle."

Letting in the Light

The common thread in all of Amanfu's work is the spiritual bent that can be traced back to those early days in church, a persuasion most clearly present in songs like "Heaven's My Home," which she co-wrote with Katie Herzig. It appears on *The Here and the Now*, in the film *The Secret Life of Bees*, and the Duhks included it on their *Migrations* album, scoring a Grammy nomination

in 2007. The song's lyrics reflect Amanfu's natural tendency to tackle not-so-easy topics.

When I was born
My daddy said I was broken
Beginning of the end
To a life I hadn't chosen
He taught me how to give up
He taught me how to work the system
But I never had the time
I never had the luxury

Herzig, a longtime friend and co-writer, has a clear view of what Amanfu brings to the table. "Mad instincts, a sense of humor, vulnerability, honesty, openness. She has a very natural way of working off and balancing out the energy of her collaborators."

"When I sit down to write a song, I have to remind myself that it's okay to be brutally honest," Amanfu says. "I definitely have a heart to lift people up, but a friend of mine told me a really important thing: You can lift people even if the subject matter you're singing or writing about is heavy, because sometimes you're giving voice to someone else's heaviness. And that makes them feel that it's lifted off of them."

In Amanfu's hands, even the hopeless have a hopefulness. All those years spent listening to the gospel of Mavis Staples and the soul of Bill Withers pour out in her own songs. "I always have a moment in my songs when it's like, 'then comes the morning,' in a symbolic way. I have songs that are heavy, but they always have that moment of lightness in them, as well."

That equation gets spun around when it comes to the love songs she and Brooker have composed. "Sam and I laugh about this: I can never write a lyric for a love song that is just all cheery. It's always, [sings] 'I love you... but sometimes you make me mad and then we fight and then I don't know.'" Amanfu laughs, then adds: "It's always, 'I love you, but.'"

Happily-ever-afters aside, Amanfu landed herself a back-up singer spot in Wanda Jackson's band on the rockabilly legend's tour supporting *The Party Ain't Over* in 2011. Because that album was produced by Jack White, the gig brought Amanfu into the Third Man fold, and, a year later, White tapped Amanfu

"You can lift people even if the subject matter you're singing or writing about is heavy, because sometimes you're giving voice to someone else's heaviness."

Ruby Amanfu

to be his vocal counterpoint on his *Blunderbuss* LP. Taking that show on the road, Amanfu spent the better part of the next two years on tour with White as part of his band.

Sneaking into studios along the way, whenever and wherever she could, she managed to pull together a solo EP, *The Simple Sessions*, produced by Charlie Peacock. And, even as she worked through all of those "day jobs," she was quietly toiling away on a full-length album with producers Mark Howard and Austin Scaggs. The mostly covers collection saw daylight last year as the stunning *Standing Still* and includes cuts by Bob Dylan, Jay Clifford, Richard Hawley, Jimmie Dale Gilmore, Brandi Carlile, and others. In their native forms, these compositions would, indeed, be hard-pressed to fit anywhere other than folk or country. Yet Amanfu infuses them with her own thing, as she wiggles her way into the heart of each song. And each of those songs wrestles with matters of faith, in one regard or another.

"I go on my gut," she explains. "But my gut is seasoned in a way that I know what message I want to get across from the podium. I have this desire to say something with a capital 'S.' … As I sit here right now, the sun is streaming in the window and I don't know how to write a full song about just that. [But] people *do*. They do it really, really well. I'm not good at that. I want to say the whys of it. … This is a lifelong thing that hasn't quite changed yet, where I feel a conviction

and a responsibility for the message I put out, whether it's a song I write or not."

It's that conviction that infuses Amanfu's artistry with compassionate spirit. There's a sense that she's "been there, done that." And, because of the depth and breadth of experiences she draws from, it feels genuine.

As Bonnie Baker sees it, "Ruby isn't bound by the social trappings that held other beautiful female artists closer to the ground that came before her. Because they paved the way, she has been able to push herself further, musically. … There really isn't a genre that she fits into. She doesn't follow rules at all, and that is what makes her Ruby."

Putting into words the spiritual experience that music can be is difficult. Is it possible, then, to describe the place a singer goes to when they are singing? Amanfu tries. "Something that comes to mind is what it feels like, for me, to go for a swim – especially me, not swimming very well at all. There's something about how you're conscious of having to stay afloat, but there's also something that is naturally overtaking – that is the water. So I often feel that I can't deny that the water is going to take me, if it wants to take me. But I'm also aware that it takes a certain skill and strength to continue to plow through it, to continue to move forward in it."

She also knows that, if you surrender to the water, it buoys you. So she surrenders herself to the music. "Being on stage has always been a hard thing

for me because it's so exposing in that way, so I have to remember … that I know what to do. I know where the notes go and how they come out."

Keeping Community

Having watched her evolve and grow for 17 years now, Brooker isn't surprised by where Amanfu is now. "I feel like she's well aware of it being a hard road," he says, "yet she's determined. It's just who she is."

Further, Amanfu appreciates her place in the tradition. "A couple years ago, I was on the Cayamo cruise, listening and watching Buddy Miller and Emmylou Harris and Rodney Crowell," she recounts. "They were talking about how they were coming up in the '70s and they all had similar, but not identical, dreams that created a community for them. And they're very much like a Rat Pack now. They all did something that made an impact in society.

"I immediately thought about my community of friends right now who have a similar desire and heart for what we do and [want] to make an impact," she adds. "There's a group of us who are similar ages and we're going to look back and be 60, and I think we're going to be able to say what Buddy and Emmylou and Rodney have said: 'I had a vision and I had determination and I wanted to put good out into the world, and that came through music.'" ∎

BORN AGAIN

With help
from friends,
Mavis Staples
takes us
there again

by Kelly McCartney

"[Pops] said, 'Mavis, guess what? They want us to open at Tabernacle Baptist Church for Sister Mahalia Jackson on Monday night.' Lord, I thought my little heart was coming out of my chest."

Mavis Staples

SIXTY-FIVE YEARS INTO HER recording career, Mavis Staples' incomparable voice and infectious spirit are truly wonders to behold.

Born in 1939 to Oceola and Roebuck "Pops" Staples, Mavis got her start early, singing in church and at home in Chicago. Pops put together a family band, and Mavis, the youngest, soon became the star of the Staple Singers. With them, she lit up the world with songs like "I'll Take You There," "Let's Do It Again," "Respect Yourself," and so many others.

Over the decades since, both the Gospel and the song have stayed intrinsically linked in her heart, even as she has spread her musical wings wide, working with an eclectic group of collaborators, from Jeff Tweedy to Joan Osborne, Prince to Patty Griffin. Though she has long released her own albums, it was 2011 before she won her first Grammy Award – Best Americana Album for the soul-stirring, Tweedy-produced *You Are Not Alone*.

But acclaim was never her game. Staples' pull to the music seems unattached to anything other than the pure pleasure and emotional expression of the music itself. If she weren't "Mavis Staples, the much-lauded gospel singer," no doubt she'd still be "Mavis, that lady with the amazing voice in the church choir." That unadulterated joy is why M. Ward, Ben Harper, Valerie June, Aloe Blacc, Justin Vernon, Neko Case, and others carved out time to write the songs for her new album, *Livin' on a High Note* (Anti- Records, Feb. 19). The set is funky and spunky and raring to go ... just like Staples herself.

KELLY McCARTNEY: You made your debut singing with the family band when you were 10, right? Obviously Pops taught you a lot, but who were your earliest influences other than him?
MAVIS STAPLES: I really loved Sister Mahalia Jackson – Sister Mahalia Jackson and Sister Rosetta Tharpe. But Mahalia was the very first female voice that I heard singing. I used to be in my little play area in the back room and I would hear Pops playing these records. He always had so many male artists – the Soul Stirrers, the Dixie Hummingbirds, the Blind Boys. All of a sudden, I heard this lady's voice and it moved me on into the living room where my father was. I sat on the floor and he said, "Mavis, you were rocking! You like that, don't you?" I said, "Yeah, daddy. Who is that?" He said, "That's Sister Mahalia Jackson." And I tell you, Pops would have to play Sister Mahalia Jackson's record for me almost every day. Every day.

I finally met her. Pops came home from work one day and said, "Mavis, guess what?" I said, "What, daddy?" He said, "They want us to open at Tabernacle Baptist Church for Sister Mahalia Jackson on Monday night." Lord, I thought my little heart was coming out of my chest. I got so excited. The bad thing about that, though, was I had to wait a weekend. This was a Friday and we weren't going until Monday. So all that weekend, I was walking around the house just singing her songs. Pops had to tell my mother, "Oce, stop the baby." [Laughs] My mother said, "Mavis, come on, baby. Rest a little bit. When you see Sister Mahalia Jackson, don't get on her nerves." I said, "I won't get on her nerves, mama."

I was so glad to meet that lady. We became friends. She would come to our house for Fourth of July. She loved my mother's homemade ice cream. She would always tell me, "Come here, baby. Get me a little more of that ice cream." I'd say, "Yes, ma'am. Yes, ma'am."

The last time I saw her was in 1969. We were on this gospel festival in New York. It was outdoors. I would make it a point always to sit next to her on stage. She leaned over to me and told me, "Baby, Halia don't feel too good. I need you to help me sing this song." I told her, "Yes, ma'am. I'll help you."

By me being a church girl, I knew what the song was when the keyboard started playing. She told me, "You go ahead. You start it." I started. The song was "Precious Lord, Take My Hand." After I did the first verse, someone helped her up to the microphone. There I was, on the same microphone with my idol and my mentor. I was so proud. I'll never forget that day.

KM: I bet. Then, though, you *did* tell Pops you wanted to play guitar like Sister Rosetta, didn't you? How'd that go?

MS: [Laughs] I sure did! That didn't go so well. He bought me a little practice guitar. He said, "Mavis, you gotta cut your fingernails off." I cut all my fingernails off and we got started. I was about 11 years old, then. Pops was still young. He was still frisky. He just didn't have the patience to teach me.

He hung with me for maybe about two and a half weeks, trying to help me. One day he told me, "Mavis, listen. You go down to Lyon & Healy and get some guitar lessons down there." I didn't know what to say! If I had been older, I would have done that. But I told him, I said, "Daddy, I want to pick it. I want to pick it like you and Sister Rosetta Tharpe." If I had been older, I would've gone to Lyon & Healy and learned, gotten some basics. Then, he could've taught me to pick it later. But I was so young. I couldn't go downtown by myself to Lyon & Healy.

The guitar was thrown out. I just couldn't. But the more and more I would see it … every little girl is playing guitar today. I tried to get my guitarist – I said, "Rick, can you give me some lessons?" He said, "Mavis, you can just strum. Just strum." I said, "I think I can do that!" So, I'm still working on it. [Laughs] I don't know. Maybe I missed my turn.

KM: I think you had another calling, is what it was.

MS: Yeah. I hear you. I better go and keep singing.

KM: Even without picking a guitar, you still follow Sister Rosetta's lead, in that you bridge the gap between gospel and rock and roll, and you continue to explore that in-between area. No matter the genre, music is a spiritual experience. So, do you feel like that combination – putting a little bit of a rock edge on these deeply meaningful songs – do you think people connect with that more so than they would if it were straight gospel?

MS: I *do*. I feel that they connect. And, being me, I don't care if I'm singing a sure-enough love song, you're gonna hear some gospel in my voice. By me being a gospel singer, I can't get away from it.

I recorded "A House Is Not a Home" years ago and I was so afraid that the church people were going to be angry with me. Turned out, the gospel radio was playing "A House Is Not a Home" on the gospel stations. So I got lucky. Nobody bothered me about recording my secular album.

But I think people *do* get it. I don't know if it would come from *anyone* singing but, by me being a gospel singer, it happens like that. I sing "The Weight." When I sing, "Take a load off, Annie," it's a difference, coming from me than a regular rock singer.

KM: There is a *little* bit of a gap between you and Levon [Helm].

MS: That's my guy! That's my guy! You know, the other day, I was cleaning a closet, and I found some drumsticks Levon had given me. Oh, I just had a fit. I propped them up in a candle holder so I can see them every day. I'm not putting them back in the closet. [Laughs]

KM: I love it!

MS: Yeah, Levon was my guy. And Levon – he and Pops were tight buddies. Levon was the only person that I know who called Pops by his name, Roebuck. Pops and my Uncle Sears. Pops' family ran out of names when they were born because they had 14 children. And they named my father's brother "Sears" and they named Pops "Roebuck." [Laughs] Everybody had that Sears Roebuck catalog down in Mississippi. So, Levon would be, "Roebuck! Roebuck!" Pops would get so tickled.

When we were doing *The Last Waltz*, Marty [Scorsese] gave us a break. We all took a break and Levon stayed on his drums – he was sitting back there on the drums. Pops walked back there and started talking to him. Pops said, "Levon, man, you smoking two cigarettes?"

Levon had one cigarette in one hand and he had his Mary Jane in the other. Levon held it up and told him, "Oh, Roebuck. You need to try this one." Pops said, "Man, I don't want that!" My sister said, "Daddy, Levon offered you a joint." He said, "I know what it was. I didn't want none!"

KM: Now, speaking of your friends. On this new record – you used to write songs, but on this one, you "got help from all the people who love" you.

MS: Yeah. I sure did!

KM: There's Ben Harper, Valerie June, Justin Vernon, Neko Case, and a whole slew of others writing songs for you. Did you offer any guidance about what types of songs you wanted or topics you wanted to explore?

MS: Oh, yes. I did. I spoke with a lot of them on the phone.

One little girl [Charity Rose Thielen from the Head and the Heart], she was just so shy, she would hardly talk to me. [Sings] "If it's a light…" – she did that one.

I talked to that little guy, too. [Sings] "Mavis, take us back. Mavis, take us back." Benjamin Booker. He's a young kid out of New Orleans. I would tell them that I wanted some songs that were happy, that were uplifting. I let them know that I've been singing sad songs and singing songs that have been telling the world about the hard times, the bad times we had during the Movement, and I wanted to come up out of that. I wanted to sing some songs that would lift you up in a different way. I didn't want to mention, but I couldn't help it, I did the "MLK Song." That was Dr. King's speech, and I remembered that speech so well. When M. Ward brought it to me, I couldn't resist it. I had to do that.

But I would tell them I wanted something joyful. This kid [Booker] came right with what I needed. "I got friends and I got people who love me." That means all of these songwriters who took time off of their busy schedules to write a song for Mavis – old Grandma Mavis! They know me. A lot of them surprised me. They know me. They have followed my work and they jumped right on it. They were happy to write for me.

I know Neko Case. She's my friend. And I know Ben Harper. This little guy, Benjamin Booker, he came to a show we had in London and I met him. I had talked with him on the phone. He started

THE STAPLE SINGERS
1420 S. Ashland Ave. Chicago, Ill.   Tel. CAnal6-8548

"I've been singing sad songs and singing songs that have been telling the world about the hard times, the bad times we had during the Movement, and I wanted to come up out of that. I wanted to sing some songs that would lift you up in a different way."

Mavis Staples

singing to me, "Mavis, take us back. Mavis, take us back." I said, "Where you wanting me to take you back to?" [Laughs]

KM: Well, you took us *there*, so you might as well take us *back*! You're the only one who can!

MS: Yeah! [Laughs] That's right! That's exactly where he was coming from!

KM: I got it!

MS: Yeah, yeah. So I *love* that song. Valerie June – I met her several times. I knew her from New York. I got so tickled when I got her song because she has this really Southern accent. She's a real cute little girl and you just wouldn't expect her to sound like that. I still have my Southern accent, but it's what we call "talking Black." That's what I do. I talk Black. [Laughs] But Valerie June, when she sent that song, I thought she was saying "leaving" because that's how it sounded – [Sings] "Leavin' on a high note. Leavin' on a high note."

[Laughs] I said, "Is she saying 'leaving' or is she saying 'living'?"

I said, "Oh, Lord. She's gonna have me saying 'leaving'!"

KM: Nope. We're not ready for you to leave yet, Mavis. Please.

MS: No! I ain't ready to go, either! But she was sending me on away from here! I was so glad that it was "Livin' on a High Note." She is beautiful. She's singing on that song, you know.

KM: Yeah. I can hear her.

MS: Yeah! Oh, she has a beautiful voice. Neko Case, "History Now," I love that song. I love all of my songs. I love them all. Ben Harper, "Love and Trust," that one kind of took me back – this is what we're still looking for: love and trust. These are much younger people than myself, and I was just so honored that these young people have been following my career and know me.

This guy that wrote for me, Aloe Blacc, I loved his voice when I first heard his record. I said, "Who is *this* guy?!" Then I started seeing him on TV shows. When the managers would ask me who I had in mind to write me a song, I said, "Definitely Aloe Blacc. Let's see if we can get one from him." He sent his in pretty early. Valerie June was first. Then Aloe Blacc came with "Tomorrow." When I did "Tomorrow," my friend Trombone Shorty came in and did a solo on that for me. He's a youngster, too, and I'm crazy about Trombone Shorty.

It's like a rebirth, Kelly. I've been born again. Everything is just blowing up! At this time in my life, I've got to be the happiest old girl in the world.

KM: It's wonderful to see, I'll tell you that.

MS: It's wonderful for me to see, too. My brother said, "Mavis, what is going *on*?!" I said, "Pervis, people *like* me!" ■

GROWING UP GOSPEL

Church inflects Anderson East's emerging voice *by Cara Gibney*

"A lot of people, especially in the South, grew up with a tradition of gospel in the church. They were surrounded by that sound and there's no way that you can separate [from] either the music or the feeling that it's supposed to invoke."

Anderson East

ANDERSON EAST SQUINTS THROUGH his cigarette smoke, smiling into the screen for a Skype conversation. It's been a wild year for the Athens, Alabama-bred singer-songwriter whose soul-drenched vocals seem to pour out of his clean-looking white-boy face. Home for a break from months of grueling touring, he's doing what singer-songwriters the world over are asked to do: take time out and explain to a reporter where his music comes from. He leans forward in his chair. Behind him sit unpacked cases. I ask him to describe his music. "All we are," he tells me between sips of coconut water, "is some kind of weird concoction of our influences and what we've been exposed to."

Gifted with a voice potent with Southern soul and gospel, East's 2015 album *Delilah* (Low Country Sound/ Elektra) was produced by Americana star-maker Dave Cobb after he'd just finished his laying of hands on break-through efforts from Jason Isbell and Sturgill Simpson. *Delilah* is steeped in those soul and gospel tones of East's voice, along with the R&B, country, and foot-tappin' rock and roll that his own Alabamian "weird concoction" has exposed him to.

Back in his Alabama childhood, East's grandfather was a Baptist preacher, his mother played piano for the local church, and his father sang in the choir. The music wasn't brought home, though. "Growing up," he says, "music wasn't a huge aspect of our family life. It got left at the church – that's where it stayed."

Still, the gospel music found its way into his voice. "I think a lot of people, especially in the South, grew up with a tradition of gospel in the church," he says. "They were surrounded by that sound and there's no way that you can separate [from] either the music or the feeling that it's supposed to invoke."

Finding a Voice

Beyond his family's church-based music-making, East's influences are not surprising once you've heard him. Without hesitation, he namechecks Joni Mitchell and Don Williams, and he's a huge fan of Emmylou Harris. He mentions Aretha Franklin and Vince Gill, he quotes Tom Waits, and one can't gloss over his love of Wilson Pickett. "There's this thing in Wilson that scares me to death," he says about the R&B/soul legend. "He's able to be manly and almost aggressive, but in the same breath, tender and gentle. He never really got the credit he deserved."

All of these influences, and more, make up the essence of the still-developing Anderson East sound. Like with Pickett, there is Alabama honey in East's voice. Pickett had shingle scraping in his, and it was part of what helped that rasp, that "manly" forcefulness that East is talking about.

East's voice has sand in there, too, though in varying amounts. You can hear this inflection on *Delilah*. The clearer tones in "What a Woman Wants to Hear"

render the singing more reminiscent of Vince Gill than Pickett. "Quit You" (co-written with Chris Stapleton), on the other hand, conjures the ghosts of sand-drenched soul – and it's not just the voice, it's the energy and elation in it. Of course he mentions Aretha Franklin, and something of that effortless gospel-tinged powerhouse appears in songs like "Find 'Em, Fool 'Em, and Forget 'Em," where East mixes soul and funk, defying you to remain still.

"I've put a lot of music in general in my head," he says. "Hopefully some of the best parts that I've learned are from singers who have their own voice. That fascinates me. It inspires me. It makes me more willing to figure out who I am and what my voice is."

Nashville songwriter Aaron Raitiere, who has worked with the Vespers and Whiskey Myers, went to school with East. Ten years into their friendship, he says they're "always working on something." So it's no surprise that he was involved in cowriting just under half of the tracks on *Delilah*.

The way Raitiere sees it, the spirit of East's music is in his bones. "I think that Anderson is a sort of vehicle for all of the collective elements of the music he is making," he says. "Kind of like the music was already made a long time ago and he is just a means of physical transmission ... All those songs were in the dirt, and the wind and the water. All we had to do was see them and dig them up, or catch them or whatever. I imagine you could ask him to do another version, but it would probably still come out smothered in undeniable gospel, soul, and spirit."

This saturation in music doesn't quite fit with the musical landscape from which East hails. Athens may be an hour's drive away from Muscle Shoals – where East recorded some tracks from *Delilah* live in FAME Studios – but growing up there actually limited his contact with live music. "There's no music community [in Athens]," he explained. "We had to go to Huntsville or Birmingham to actually see a show. I remember going to my first one and my mind being blown."

It's an environment hard to imagine for the singer, songwriter, musician, and gearhead that Anderson East is today. "It's a strange thing," he shrugs. "I don't want to use the word 'deprived,' but I can't think of a better adjective for what it was. You always want something you can't have," he says, grinning.

As a result, East had no exact musical compass. "I had no basis of what was cool at all," he remembers. "My buddy's sister gave me a Grateful Dead record and I hadn't even heard of them, so it was awesome to check them out. Everything was a precious commodity. Anything we as kids could get our hands on, we were just so apt to soak it in, whatever it was."

Going for Gear

East was ten years old when he started learning guitar. His father organized lessons that lasted about a year, but those petered out. The same proved true when his mother sent him to learn piano. "I was just so infatuated with [music] that I didn't need anybody to tell me how to do it," he recalls, adding, "I was never one of those kids that could copy a guitar solo. I would know the first few bars of a tune and then from there I was clueless. I just decided I was going to start writing songs myself."

Soon, he got his hands on a four-track tape recorder and he hit the sweet spot. A fledgling gearhead was born. "You can cue [the four-track] and it has some effects," he remembers. "It was a really cool thing, and I was hooked." He went on to study sound engineering, and at age 19 he moved to Nashville, where he worked in various studios, learning on the job

from some of the town's finest sound engineers. After a spell, he got work recording demos for up-and-coming bands, eventually opening his own studio.

"Me and my guitar player Scotty [Murray] started the studio on the bottom floor of this house," he says, referring to his close friend and the band's director, guitar player, and sometimes preacher.

"Anderson moved in with us about [four or five] years ago when he was a tender little shoot," Murray says. "We decided to turn the bottom floor of the house into a recording studio pretty much immediately after Anderson rolled in. He turned out to be a pretty good engineer."

Slowly but surely, all this time, doors were opening for East. Among them was playing guitar and singing for Holly Williams, when she was out promoting her critically acclaimed 2013 release, *The Highway*. "That was my only gig as a sideman," he says. "She asked me, 'Can you play guitar and sing?' and I was like, 'Yes! Absolutely.' I was so broke at the time I was like, 'I can do anything.'"

The next door that opened was after a gig that East played at Nashville's storied Bluebird Café, when producer Dave Cobb introduced himself. The pair hit it off immediately, not least because of some pretty useful shared interests, and they've since gone on to become firm friends – which East finds essential in his work.

"I developed such a trust with that guy," East explains. "Anytime I had tried to work with somebody else, another engineer or producer, I always felt like I needed some type of hand in that process, on the technical side. So I couldn't focus on being the person behind the microphone. With Dave it was like, 'Okay, I'm letting my guard down. I have full trust in you and whatever comes out is what it is.'"

While East attributes a mutual affection for recording gear to the reason he and Cobb hit it off so well, Cobb references their shared taste in the way records were made back in the day. "I think we're both attracted to the looseness, danger, and the human feel on those records." Cobb says. "When I hear old Little Richard or Otis Redding, they weren't going for perfection, they were just trying to make you *feel*."

Anyone digging into East's Cobb-produced record can hear that

determination to make you feel, and Cobb's appreciation of what comes over when East sings was central to the recording process. "He has such an amazing voice," Cobb says. "He's the real deal vocally – that's why I wanted to work with him. All I was trying to do was frame the music to stay out of the way."

Murray can vouch for the way Cobb's approach to East's music made all the difference. "I hadn't had a chance to hear what they were cooking up," he says, "but I figured it was good by the way it made Anderson act like a superhero. He called me from the studio one night. They were finishing vocals on a tune and he drank way too much to drive home. When I arrived, they were listening to his last take on 'Find 'Em, Fool 'Em, and Forget 'Em.' It was the funkiest thing I'd heard in ages. I thought, no wonder he's acting like a superhero."

The album dropped last July, and a heavy tour schedule that had already included opening spots with Brandi Carlile, the Lone Bellow, John Butler Trio, and others ramped up. East's all-out, animated performance onstage is becoming his signature. It's a lot of fun for East, who has old friends like Murray in the band. But it can be hard too, as Murray explains. "Being an opening act … we quickly realized how hard it is to get the attention of a crowd that doesn't know you and didn't come to see you. We'd eventually get them, but it would take three to four songs before they realized they needed to get involved."

For East it was a double-sided coin. "Our live show is really high energy, a lot of running around. But so much touring, it's all output. You're just trying to give as much as you can. And survive. So there wasn't a lot of input being put back in. It's like Bukowski says: 'It's hard to feed without getting fed.'"

Of course, that was last year. He says 2016 is the year he'll exercise more and quit smoking. This is the year for more writing, he says, taking advantage of that "weird concoction" of his.

"I'm more excited than I think I've ever been, writing songs again and making a new record," he says, peering into Skype. "I'm hoping it's going to be as good as I imagine it. I just want to explore myself and my personality a lot more and in a different manner. I'm ready to find my sound – that's what it is." ∎

LAND OF THE RISING SOUND

Tokyo-based mandolinist Inoue Taro.

**Exploring bluegrass
and authenticity
in Japan** *by Denis Gainty*

What is it about our national identity that feeds into bluegrass? Why should making a certain kind of sound be tied to what we look like, what language we speak, or where we're from? And how, for both Japanese and Americans, do these questions affect the way we respond to the idea of bluegrass music in Japan?

I ARRIVE AT THE FESTIVAL LATE IN the afternoon. It's August 2013, and the sun is still high in the sky when I get out of the car, stretch my legs, and walk with my new friend Kaz up the slope from the grassy parking area. Kaz's stately, long Jaguar stands out in the parking lot of compacts and micro-compacts, battered pickup trucks, and shiny minivans. He's carrying his guitar, and I have my mandolin, my backpack, and a camera. I check in at the lodge at the top of the parking area and pay for the luxury of a dorm-style room with air conditioning. Walking farther, we pass cleared dirt campsites where large, open tents have already been set up. While small children run shrieking around, twenty-something adults in folding chairs gather around makeshift cooking areas. Further up the hill, the path cuts to the left and passes a large stage, where workers bustle around with microphone cables and other gear. Camp chairs and blankets dot the terraced hillside, and an imposing wooden lodge looms on the right. In the dim interior of the lodge, I can see college students milling around institutional-sized cooking vats. A long table at the front of the lodge advertises food, soda, and beer for sale. I smell meat.

I drop my bag in my room, take a moment to appreciate the window overlooking the mountain pond, and join Kaz to walk further up the hill. He greets other festivalgoers with a quiet, serious word. He tells me as we walk about a young group from North Carolina at the festival this year; I should enjoy talking to them, he says. He points out one of the two brothers who founded the festival in 1972, making it the world's second longest-running bluegrass festival in continuous operation. It's a point of pride that only Bill Monroe's Bean Blossom festival has been operating for longer.

I wave to a luthier I met earlier that week, and he walks over to chat. He knows Kaz; everyone knows Kaz. I promise to come back later, and we continue up the hill. Finally, we reach a small clearing where several camps have been set and a fire has been lit, anticipating the cool mountain evening. Kaz introduces me to another luthier – an imposing older man with a sharp nose, cropped white hair, and sunglasses. He hands Kaz a new mandolin with a bold, emerald-green finish over beautifully flamed maple. I introduce myself, and tell him that I'm a history professor from Georgia.

"Oh really?" he says.

I tell him I'm conducting research for a book on the history of bluegrass music in Japan.

"Oh really!" he repeats, but this time he smiles.

This is my first Japanese bluegrass festival – high on a hilltop with almost a thousand other bluegrass fans in Hyogo Prefecture, in Sanda, north of the city of Takarazuka from which the festival takes its name. While this is undisputedly the king of Japanese festivals – founded by the brothers Watanabe Toshio and Inoue (Watanabe) Saburo, members of the trailblazing Japanese bluegrass band Bluegrass 45 – it's one of a great many that take place annually in Japan, from the northernmost island of Hokkaido to the southern reaches of Okinawa. Like the settings in which they're held, festivals range in character from the familiar camping, picking, socializing model of American festivals like Bean Blossom to ad hoc meetings in urban parks, suburban community centers, and university dormitory common areas. Like American festivals, most are held from May to October, drawing crowds of various ages and backgrounds. And like American festivals, they are at least as much a chaotic celebration of the bluegrass community – of the social meaning of bluegrass in the lives of the people who love it – as they are a formal exercise in listening to live music.

But despite the similarities – or perhaps because of them – the Japanese bluegrass community is, for an American observer, a delightful dip into the unique blend of familiar and strange that turn-of-the-century German psychologist Ernst Jentsch called the uncanny. Things at Takarazuka – and at Asagiri, Tokushima, Yakumo, and the other festivals I've had the pleasure of attending in Japan – sound and feel so close to my experience with bluegrass festivals at American campgrounds. They carry the same serendipitous movement from picking circle to picking circle until and beyond daybreak, the same happy greetings, the same invitations to share food and drink around a fire. A Lester Flatt G-run on a Martin D-28 guitar sounds the same in Ginza as in Galax. Close your eyes, shut out the smells of dashi and yakisoba, and you could be anywhere in the States, listening to high, lonesome odes to rural innocence, times gone by, parents deceased, moonshine brewed, lovers murdered, and trains.

Then, of course, the little discontinuities creep in – the stereotypical but real swapping of R's and L's, the odd shaping of vowels, and the occasional, phonetically learned nonsense lyric. Still, most singers in Japanese bluegrass are expert at producing the classic high, lonesome sound. When non-native English accents emerge, then, it's all the more jarring against what is almost pure Appalachia. Like Mick Jagger's carefully crafted American blues diction – or, for that matter, like Jessye Norman's Italian in *Aida*, or Placido Domingo's Russian in *Eugene Onegin* – Japanese bluegrass vocals are tuned to producing a non-native sound. To be sure, some of this tuning is from familiarity.

My friend Kaz – Inaba Kazuhiro, one of the very few Japanese bluegrassers who have made a successful career as a professional musician – has spent a great deal of time in Virginia, North Carolina, and other Eastern American mountain states. His fluent English has an organically acquired Appalachian twang. Inoue Taro, a genre-bending mandolin player in Tokyo and son of festival organizer, bluegrass pioneer, and banjo picker Inoue Saburo, speaks the profanity-laden near-native English he acquired during his time as a college student in East Tennessee State University's bluegrass program. But most Japanese bluegrass musicians have only high-school English, a close pedagogical cousin to the near-universal failure that is Spanish language instruction in American public schools. Many have never been to the United States. And despite this, most sound almost perfectly American.

This linguistic variation at the edge of Japanese bluegrass vocals captures the basic sense that Japanese bluegrass is just slightly out of alignment. When I first encountered Japanese bluegrass in 1993, in a small town south of Osaka, I had only recently arrived in Japan. I had almost no Japanese language, and I was feeling increasingly far from home. The sounds of a bluegrass band at a local izakaya, or pub, should have been a welcome reminder of home, comforting me in an otherwise strange setting, soothing my culture shock. And of course they were. But at the same time, there was something disturbing, brought about precisely because those songs – "Rolling in my Sweet Baby's Arms," "Nine Pound Hammer," "Blackberry Blossom" – were so familiar. My confusion was heightened when I went to congratulate and thank the band, and discovered that several of them – including the guitarist who'd been belting out such sweet, high tenor vocals – didn't speak English.

Americans on Parade

It's not just the language that marks Japanese bluegrass as somehow different from its American cousin. Some of the differences are rooted in culture; others are simply quirks. At the 2013 Takarazuka festival, the Kobe University student-run kitchen was the only food and drink for sale, and the nearest store was a four-mile hike away. Upon waking up the first morning, I learned that there was no coffee to be had, and aside from packaged snack foods, beef over rice – gyudon – was the only food item for breakfast, lunch, and dinner. Okay, I thought, what the hell. I ordered gyudon for breakfast.

After a pained silence, a student told me apologetically that the beef wouldn't be ready until 11 a.m.

"What is there?" I asked.

The student looked helpfully with me at the posted, handwritten menu.

"There's ... um, beer?"

Along with beer for breakfast, Japanese festivals offer a more democratic approach than their American counterparts. Partly due to the relative scarcity of professional bluegrassers in Japan, the typical festival lineup includes literally dozens, and sometimes more than a hundred, acts. The usual set is 10 to 15 minutes, and the resulting effect is less that of a concert than of a small-town variety show. Everyone, it seems, is welcome to participate; the emphasis is on community more than expertise.

At Takarazuka, the stage is a constant bustle of activity from mid-morning to well past midnight, as acts cycle on and off, laughing and joking together, striking up tunes they'd just played, or were about to play again, in one of the innumerable jam circles. The distinction between audience and performer is, for the most part, a joyful mess.

At the same time, there's a palpable heightening of attention and energy when American acts take the stage. At the Takarazuka festival, some of the loudest applause was reserved for American performers like the North Carolina trio Mipso and Anya Hinkle, fiddler and vocalist for the Asheville group Tellico. Mipso's mandolin player, Jacob Sharp, first visited Japan as a University of North Carolina undergraduate in 2012, and he brought his band for a return visit in 2013. Hinkle had traveled south to the festival with her husband and child from her husband's native home in Hokkaido. Both were greeted with thunderous applause from what had been a relatively reserved crowd.

Crowds at Japanese festivals – at any Japanese bluegrass performance – are not exactly quiet, but they don't whoop quite like Americans do. During a 2013 performance at the Tokyo club Back in Town by the immensely talented Berklee College alumnus Arita Hiro (Yoshihiro), I gave a holler after a particularly juicy solo. Heads turned. A couple of songs later, Arita explained helpfully to the crowd – almost entirely Japanese, male, and over 50 – that at bluegrass shows in America, it was customary to make noise outside the designated applause periods. Several Japanese men turned and smiled at me approvingly, and one gave me a thumbs-up.

This and other experiences made me feel like some kind of cultural authority was conferred simply by my American identity. The same year, I attended a show at Moonstomp, a club in western Tokyo. The mandolin player interrupted the set to call attention to my presence in the crowd, and then invited me to explain for everyone the meaning of the English word "jubilee."

Both as performers and audience members, then, it seems that the presence of real live Americans carries a sort of cachet for Japanese bluegrassers – a peg onto which to hang the collective hat of authenticity. This speaks to a basic question: what is it about our national identity that feeds into bluegrass? Why should making a certain kind of sound be tied to what we look like, what language we speak, or where we're from? And how, for both Japanese and Americans, do these questions affect the way we respond to the idea of bluegrass music in Japan?

With a few exceptions, both American and Japanese players and fans seem acutely conscious of bluegrass's American identity. In American settings, this can come out in overt ways – American flags or patriotically-themed caps or T-shirts, for example – but we don't need to hear the word "Americana" or the Jim and Jesse McReynolds song "Thank God for the USA" to know that bluegrass is American. What marks bluegrass in the States, much of the time, is the undertone of nostalgia and belonging generated by an implicit reference to an authentically American past.

Bluegrass is, in many ways, the theme song to the modern economic history of the United States. Born of a Depression-era labor diaspora from rural Appalachia

"Like jazz or classical music, bluegrass is universal music ... the kind of music [that transcends] country, race, religion, and language."

Inoue Saburo

North Carolina-based bluegrass band Mipso
in front of Ginkaku-ji temple in Kyoto.

to Southeastern (and then further-flung) urban centers, the popularization of bluegrass's immediate ancestors – known as "hillbilly music," "mountain music," or by other names – served a paradoxical desire to communicate rural authenticity to a displaced, urban population that longed for a home that never was. Bluegrass musicians employed modern technologies and emerging capitalist networks to evoke a feeling of family-centered stringband simplicity at a neighbor's farmhouse.

That these audiences were mostly white Protestants largely unaware of the profound African-American influences on their favorite musical stylings is itself reflective of so much American history. In the same way, it's also reflective of America's diversity and inclusivity that bluegrass's modern popularity is based so clearly in the folk music boom of the 1950s in New York City, when disenchanted Americans – usually college-educated, urban, and often Jewish – began to celebrate bluegrass as a genuine American tradition. Folklorists and enthusiasts like Moses Asch, John and Alan Lomax, Mike and

Pete Seeger, and Ralph Rinzler labored to codify and communicate "authentic" American music, even as they helped to create a new, sophisticated web of production and consumption.

Banjo Diplomacy

In this sense, it's hard not to see bluegrass as American, and its presence in Japan as evidence of American influence. If so, it's warmly welcomed. As the historian Neil Rosenberg noted in his 1985 study of bluegrass, there is no country outside North America in which bluegrass has found more of a home than Japan. Along with the many annual festivals, countless live venues dedicated to bluegrass and related genres are found across the country. At universities from Hokkaido to Okinawa, students gather in bluegrass circles – many with impressive names like "American Traditional Music Research Society" – to explore and celebrate the music together. Various periodicals include the monthly bluegrass publication *Moonshiner*, produced by Inoue Saburo, who, with his brother Watanabe Toshio,

also runs the internet-based mail-order outfit B.O.M. (Bluegrass and Old-Time Music) Services.

In some ways, too, it makes sense that an American musical form would put down roots all over the world, and especially in Japan. America's modern cultural dominance is well documented, and it's no longer surprising to find Kentucky Fried Chicken in Moscow or to see NBA jerseys in South Africa. But bluegrass roots in Japan go to the very beginning of American efforts to stretch beyond its borders and flex its imperial muscles.

As Saburo – Sab to his many bluegrass friends – is fond of pointing out, the one-and-a-half-century-long American presence in Japan began with the banjo. In 1853, the naval officer Matthew Calbraith Perry, veteran of the War of 1812 and other conflicts, sailed with his small fleet of ultra-modern steam warships into Edo (now Tokyo) Bay. With guns trained on the port of Uraga, Perry communicated to the shogunate – Japan's military government, ruling in the name of the hereditary sovereign in Kyoto – the suggestion that Japan might like to sign a treaty allowing the United States access to Japanese ports. The following year, Perry returned to Japan with an even larger force – a quarter of the entire American navy at that time – and Japan signed the first of a series of treaties with foreign powers.

All of this was momentous in world history. For Japan, the intrusion of American force meant the end of roughly two centuries of carefully limited international relations. Within 15 years, Japan's hereditary military government was replaced by a modern, constitutional monarchy; within 25 years, Japan had built its own steamships and was using Perry's tactics to force its neighbor Korea into trade agreements.

But for our purposes, all this is background noise to the major event of 1854: celebrating the signing of the first Japanese-American treaty,

There's a palpable heightening of attention and energy when American acts take the stage. At the Takarazuka festival, some of the loudest applause was reserved for American performers like the North Carolina trio Mipso and Anya Hinkle, fiddler and vocalist for the Asheville group Tellico.

Commodore Perry and his Japanese counterparts arranged a series of gifts and entertainment. For the American sailors, Japanese officials presented an exhibition of sumo wrestling, hoping to impress their guests. For the Japanese, the Americans assembled and operated a one-quarter-scale steam locomotive with 350 feet of track. And to the reported delight of all concerned, the American sailors put on a blackface minstrel show, complete with fiddles, percussion, and banjos. In one fell swoop, America's brand of racially imbalanced power structures and the banjo – originating in Africa! – came to Japan.

According to one source, Perry told the crew that "the success of his treaty depended on the success of the entertainment" for the Japanese dignitaries. By this measure, the banjo was effective well beyond Perry's fondest dreams. Catalyzed by the American intrusion, the newly formed Japanese government itself began to reach beyond its borders to engage with and learn from the modern West. The Japanese government sent scores of young men to America and Europe, charged with studying government, military, and other matters.

In 1870s Boston, the young Isawa Shuji studied with Luther Mason, then America's premiere music educator, and under Mason's influence introduced a number of Christian hymns and Western songs to the Japanese national curriculum. Many of these, including

the American school song "Lightly Row" and the Scottish anthem "Auld Lang Syne," popularized by Robert Burns, were given Japanese lyrics deemed more appropriate to Japan's national ethos; however, the melodies remained, and began a reshaping of Japanese musical sensibilities that would continue through the present day. (The tune of "Auld Lang Syne," known in Japan as "Hotaru no Hikari" [Light of the Firefly] is still well known there as a signal for closing time at stores and other establishments.)

Many Japanese bluegrass fans point to the early exposure to Western scales and harmonies as a reason for bluegrass' success in what is a quintessentially non-Western society. Following the rapid transformation of Japanese society at the turn of the 20th century, American music – especially jazz – began to gain popularity until World War II, when American and British music was officially discouraged in favor of German songs and Italian operas.

Following the war, however, American musical influence came back with a vengeance. This, broadly, took two forms. The first was radio. Even before the world's first nuclear attacks incinerated much of the cities of Hiroshima and Nagasaki – and before the unthinkably intimate radio address by the Showa emperor Hirohito himself announcing the unconditional surrender of the Empire of Japan to American forces – hillbilly music was inexorably wafting through the Pacific air.

Shortly after the Japanese air attack on United States naval forces at Pearl Harbor, Hawaii, in December 1941, the first Armed Forces Radio broadcasts began in the Aleutian Islands. These broadcasts became common throughout the Pacific Islands, made available both through official broadcasting centers and via an ad hoc network of 50-watt transmitters placed at the top of palm trees by intrepid Marines – often before an island was fully wrested from Japanese control. The first Marine station, located in the Solomon Islands, used an indigenous Solomon Islander version of the 1939 hillbilly tune "You Are My Sunshine" as its signature song to open every broadcast, marking both the popularity of hillbilly music and one instance of its absorption and interpretation by non-American musicians. As US forces moved north through the Pacific Islands, they continued to set up a series of medium-wave stations comprising the so-called "Mosquito Network" and broadcasting a variety of news, spoken word, religious programming, and musical entertainment – again including indigenous Solomon Islander musical groups, who performed both Anglican hymns and secular songs such as "Humonderange" ("Home on the Range") and "Cummin Round the Montan."

Following the 1945 surrender of Japanese forces, the Mosquito Network

As Saburo is fond of pointing out, the one-and-a-half-century-long American presence in Japan began with the banjo.

was largely dissolved, and occupying American military forces were served instead by broadcasts using the infrastructure of the Nippon Hoso Kyokai (Japanese Broadcasting Corporation, known today as NHK). Under the banner of "democratization," the Allied Occupation – under Gen. Douglas MacArthur – reformulated NHK broadcasts to include popular songs, game shows, informational programs, and political debates. Many NHK facilities were taken over outright by Occupation forces, who established the Far East Network (FEN), broadcasting from Tokyo, Osaka, and other major cities. Intended for American personnel, these broadcasts included popular American radio shows and music, but also locally produced programs by US occupation musicians. "Hillbilly music" was particularly popular; according to a 1947 issue of the military publication *Pacific Stars and Stripes*, the Osaka program "Cowboy Clem" received more fan mail than any other show. On the flagship FEN station WVTR in Tokyo, programs such as "Honshu Hayride" and "Chuck Wagon Time" broadcasted hillbilly music to the nation's capital and surrounding regions.

As American forces demanded, produced, and consumed hillbilly music, it was of course also made available to Japanese listeners. From at least 1947, Japanese hillbilly groups such as the Western Melodians, the Western Ramblers, and the Chuck Wagon Boys played American hillbilly music – often with lyrics learned phonetically – for American audiences. The popularity of Western films at the time also helped to generate broad if unfocused interest on folksy, country-ish American music –

for lack of more precise adjectives – but the inclusion of "hillbilly" music in the general mix is clear.

In October 1958, the first Japanese bluegrass group – the East Mountain Boys – was formed under the guidance of American music fan Arita Tatsuo. Arita, who had organized the first American Folk Music Society in Osaka in 1956, brought together musicians Sano Sohei ("Don Sano"), the brothers Ozaki Yasushi and Ozaki Hisashi, and other veterans from earlier Japanese bands with names like Foggy Mountain Boys and Tennessee Shanty Boys. These bands consisted largely of students at Doshisha and Ritsumeikan universities in Kyoto, whose well-to-do prewar childhoods were already attuned to American music. Through playing for Occupation forces, Japanese musicians began to acquire a more polished sense of American hillbilly and related musics.

It's significant, and maybe surprising, that a supposedly traditional American musical form like bluegrass would take hold in Japan just after World War II. During MacArthur's occupation, Japanese national traditions around a divine emperor and a proud and self-sacrificing warrior culture were actively discouraged. For the Allies, Japanese national traditions were largely seen as problematic, and replacing bushido with banjos seemed like a great idea. But cultural transmission is always a two-way street; MacArthur struggled mightily to encourage Christianity, for example, with almost no success.

One clue to Japan's fondness for bluegrass is found in a closer look at exactly *which* Japanese were tuning into the Grand Ole Opry, watching American Westerns, and buying secondhand

instruments from American GIs. Bluegrass historians – including the dean of Western musical folklore studies in Japan, Mitsui Toru – note that most early Japanese bluegrassers were from relatively wealthy families. This trend continued throughout the 1960s and '70s, and Japanese bluegrass players and fans grew from a population of largely college-educated, upper-middle-class urbanites. From the late '60s, those young Japanese began to associate folk music and acoustic instruments with a growing political and social consciousness, pushing back against the perceived materialism of the 1950s and early 1960s. Faced with the ongoing American military presence in Japan, American involvement in the Vietnam conflict, and the global leftist movement of the 1960s, young Japanese saw acoustic music as symbolic of populist authenticity.

This should all seem pretty familiar to Americans. Like so-called "citybillies" and folklorists active in American cities, colleges, and universities, educated Japanese urbanites were consciously appropriating bluegrass and related folk musics as a way to express the twin ideas of dissatisfaction with consumerist modernity and a yearning for "authenticity." In January 1970, the already successful Takaishi Tomoya abandoned the Brothers Four/Kingston Trio-inspired Japanese folk scene to seek the roots of folk music in the United States. After months of travel and inspired by artists such as Bill Monroe and the Carter Family, he returned to Japan, and in 1971 founded the Backstep Country Band, later renamed The Natarsher Seven, for Takaishi's hometown of Natasho in Fukui Prefecture, north of Kyoto.

A group of college students at the annual bluegrass festival in Yakumo, Hokkaido.

This emphasis on authenticity was curiously combined, however, with Japanese lyrics. Unlike most bands then (and since!), the Natarsher Seven not only wrote their own songs in the traditional American style, but also translated songs such as "Bury Me Beneath the Willow," made famous by the Carter Family in 1927.

When I spoke with former Seven member Shirota Junji – still an active musician in Ireland and Japan – he was unequivocal about the band's significance. "The most important concept," he said, "was singing in Japanese and playing in the bluegrass and old-time styles."

And if it's odd to imagine that Japanese would seek authentic, traditional qualities from a national culture not their own, it might help to remember that the famous American folklorist Moses Asch was himself a Polish immigrant, and that Mike Seeger – half-brother to Pete and the creator of the first bluegrass LP in 1957 – learned about "traditional" American music from his musicologist father, his composer mother, and their African-

American maid, Elizabeth Cotten. Granted, the Ozaki brothers Yasushi and Hisashi might not have a clear sense of what life was like back in the holler when they listened to American mountain music in secret, in a closet, despite fears of arrest by Japan's military police. They may not have perfectly shared Bill Monroe's vision of a "Little Community Church" when, lacking instruments in the immediate postwar years of anxious scarcity, they built their own from cigar boxes and shamisen strings. But neither, perhaps, did the Boston-born, Philips Exeter and Amherst College alumnus and banjo pioneer Bill Keith, nor the New Jersey fiddler Gene Lowinger.

As an added wrinkle, it was a combination of these two non-Appalachian groups, united in their interest in authentic American music, that brought Japanese bluegrass to America. In 1970, Charles R. "Dick" Freeland, the owner of Rebel Records and a bluegrass fan from suburban Washington, DC, visited Japan in order to explore business possibilities there. While in Japan, Freeland heard the young Kobe-based group Bluegrass

45, including the brothers Toshio and Sab, and organized their US tour in 1971. The tour, including a stop at Bill Monroe's Bean Blossom Bluegrass Festival in Brown County, Indiana, introduced Japanese players to the American bluegrass community. When Toshio and Sab returned to Japan with tapes of various festivals, from the staid to the outrageous, they used those sources as inspiration to create one of Japan's first bluegrass festivals at Takarazuka in 1972.

Reception of this kind of quest for authenticity is complex. At the 2014 meeting of the International Bluegrass Music Association (IBMA), I asked Pete Wernick, past president of the IBMA and banjoist for Hot Rize, about his own experiences with Japanese bluegrass, both in Japan and in the United States. He noted with some ambivalence Bluegrass 45's performance at Carlton Haney's 1971 festival at Camp Springs, North Carolina, immortalized in the film *Bluegrass Country Soul*.

"It was instantly clear how talented and well-studied they were," Wernick

Top: Ohno Makoto teaching the author how to play "Big Mon." Bottom L to R: Sakamoto Yoshie and Sasabe Masuo of Tokyo group the Blueside of Lonesome.

said. "But then they delivered, in its entirety, one of the Country Gentlemen's main pieces of original stage shtick. ... Everyone thought it was the cutest and most amazing thing in the world. I don't know what Charlie Waller thought of it."

For Wernick, the fact that the Country Gentlemen were appearing at the same festival made it all the more problematic: "Copying is a Japanese thing," he added, "and we understand it's based on respect. But they just weren't aware of our very different norms regarding imitation." On the other hand, Wernick was quick to note, "They did it extremely well."

Wernick's comments give another, crucial perspective into the troubled celebration of authenticity that is bluegrass. Much like Monroe's famously negative reaction to the early success and attention Lester Flatt and Earl Scruggs received, even the sincerest forms of flattery can feel like unwanted imitation.

Indeed, even before the genre acquired its official name in the mid-1950s, bluegrass was celebrated for its authenticity by listeners and participants from both within – and maybe more often beyond – its original, Appalachian, Bill Monroe-centered community. This celebration of "authentic" bluegrass represents its own kind of claim about how bluegrass can and should be defined – a sort of well-meaning rhetorical power grab by East Coast urban intellectuals, folklorists, radio DJs, record company executives, and festival promoters. Moreover, within these efforts to define authentic bluegrass, the definitions of inside and outside, authentic and imitator, have shifted considerably. It now seems quaint at best that Monroe referred onstage to Gene Lowinger as "our Jewish cowboy" – a practice abandoned at Lowinger's request.

Chewing on Rawhide

For Americans and Japanese both, then, bluegrass often tends to signify

This, I've come to realize, is what happens without fail when I play bluegrass with Japanese players. As much as I'm trying to learn about bluegrass in Japan, I'm learning instead about bluegrass, period.

something particularly and authentically American. But this isn't always the case. When I visited Inoue Saburo at his home in Takarazuka a year after attending his festival in 2014, my own assumptions about national identity and bluegrass were regularly turned upside down. Part of this might have been the sheer, zany energy that is Sab. He's a lean, handsome man in his mid-60s, sharp-witted and well-read, with a ready if sardonic smile. He invited me to stay in his home, like so many itinerant bluegrass musicians and fans have before. Jerry Douglas has been there, he says, and so has Peter Rowan. At the 2015 FreshGrass festival in Massachusetts, Rowan remembered Sab fondly. When I asked Tim O'Brien in 2014 about his experience with Japanese bluegrass, his first response was, "Do you know Sab? You should talk to him."

I showed up at the train station and walked with Sab the short distance to the small apartment he shares with his wife, children, and sometimes his mother-in-law. In that short walk, he talked about his lack of a car, the current issue of the bluegrass periodical *Moonshiner* that he publishes, and the ideas of his favorite 19th-century Japanese philosophers. It was lucky, he said, that his daughter was out of town, as now I'd have a room to sleep in. I got the strong sense that he hadn't really worried much about that detail either way.

The next day, I found myself hurrying after Sab as he strode through the crowds in Osaka's Umeda Station, on his way to teach his bluegrass fiddle class. I had brought my mandolin along, just in case. And even though I'm used to the sheer profusion of shops, restaurants, exits, entrances, turnstiles, advertisements,

vending machines, and human beings moving in every direction through the multi-level, maze-like structures that are urban Japanese train stations, I was having a hard time keeping up. Sab darted suddenly to the side and almost disappeared down a small escalator, and I caught up just as he stepped into a small shop whose windows, I realized, were full of acoustic instruments. Inside, he was delivering a handful of CDs from his backpack, and I realized he was making a side delivery for the B.O.M. mail-order CD service that he and his brother Toshio operate alongside *Moonshiner*.

I was looking at a nice 1950s Gibson F-4 mandolin while Sab talked, and then suddenly he was off again, and I had to rush to catch up. More twists and turns, and then we stopped in a small food court, several levels – who knows how many – underground. We ate ikayaki, a sort of crepe with squid pieces that's one of the specialties of the Osaka area. Like many from the region, Sab's obviously proud of his roots there. The minute we finished eating, we were off again.

A few breathless minutes later, we had somehow left the station, but I didn't notice where. We rushed along city streets and then into the kind of slightly dingy office building characteristic of Osaka. If Tokyo is like New York, then Osaka is Japan's Chicago. It's a rough-around-the-edges merchant's capital, where warmth, humor, and food are more highly valued than manners or aesthetics or status.

I followed Sab into the tiny elevator – another specialty of Japan, where physical closeness with strangers is taken for granted on subways, in department stores, and almost everywhere – and

we emerged into a corridor that led to an office suite. We used this tiny windowless conference room, barely fitting five small chairs, for Sab's class.

The participants all seemed to be professionals in their 50s, maybe 60s, with classical violin training and a passion for bluegrass. They were welcoming when Sab introduced me, but intent on learning, and we dove in. "Okay, everyone," Sab said, in Japanese – "let's play 'Back Up and Push.'" And they were off, as I realized, to my shame, that it was another Bill Monroe tune that I, a supposed mandolin player, didn't know. I picked up the chords, more or less, and when it was my turn to play a break, I did my best to sketch out something melodic. The same thing happened again and again, with "Rawhide," with "Wheel Hoss," with "Dusty Miller" – whatever they chose, it turned out I'd heard it, but didn't really know it. I – the American – grew up imitating David Grisman and Sam Bush, not learning until much later about the bluegrass at the heart of it all.

At Sab's bluegrass jam class the following night, his students played and sang "Are You Washed in the Blood of the Lamb" and "I Saw the Light," but I was too wrapped up in trying to learn the songs to think about how strange it was to hear Christian hymns from Japanese.

And this, I've come to realize, is what happens without fail when I play bluegrass with Japanese players. As much as I'm trying to learn about bluegrass in Japan, I'm learning instead about bluegrass, period.

Last summer, I visited the Kyoto University bluegrass circle, and the club's leader – a Ph.D. student researching

Indian religions named Kanabishi Akihiro – was kind and patient enough to teach me "Cherokee Shuffle." I learned "Big Mon" from Ohno Makoto – a recent graduate of Kobe University and the former head of their student bluegrass club – at the annual Tokushima Bluegrass Festival, hastily relocated to a nearby community center thanks to a sudden rainstorm.

I still haven't learned "Rawhide," although my good friend Honma Masatoshi – mandolin player for the band Nessie Expedition and co-founder of Japan's first bluegrass magazine, *June Apple*, in 1973 – has generously played it for me more times than I'd like to admit. It was Masatoshi who, in his converted garage space man-cave in suburban Tokyo, surprised me with the gift of an authenticated chunk of wood from Uncle Pen's cabin, where Bill Monroe lived and learned much of the basis for his musical style. My supposed authenticity as an American, based on the flimsy foundation of my national origin and cultural roots, may be easily exposed – but at the same time, I'm acutely aware that in these experiences, the songs and sounds and meaning of bluegrass are being passed on, kept alive, by folks who live within sight of a very different set of mountains.

For Sab, in fact, the question of national identity has never had much traction. As he puts it energetically and regularly, to anyone who will listen: "Bluegrass is not American music – it's my music! ... Like jazz or classical music, bluegrass is universal music ... the kind of music [that transcends] country, race, religion, and language."

For Sab, his first experience with bluegrass was itself tied to something transcendental, beautiful, and close to home. He heard his first bluegrass tune, "The Old Hometown" in his early teens: "I still remember the day very well," he says. "The light-green waves of [the] rice field from my window where I can see the grove of the village shrine – such beauty ...

not American, [but] very Japanese!" From then, Sab tried to copy Earl Scruggs' banjo picking – "not to imitate, but to learn!" – and, following the success of Bluegrass 45 and his work in establishing the Takarazuka festival, *Moonshiner*, and the B.O.M. mail-order music service, he began to spend at least some time every year in the United States. From his position as secretary of the IBMA in 1995, he was able to spread the gospel of universal bluegrass. As Sab puts it: "I said on the board meeting, 'Sorry guys, but bluegrass is not an American music anymore!' The board members' mouths were fully open."

But what about the English lyrics, I asked – the model church, the blood of the lamb? Doesn't that mark the music as American, even for Japanese folks? And while they're at it, doesn't that seem odd to Japanese singers – that they're professing a very Christian notion of this world and the next? As a rule, Japanese singers tend to shrug this off. If they give the question any thought, it's clearly for my benefit.

At Sab's class, one student told me patiently, as if to a child: "Here in Japan, we are Buddhist or Shinto. So we don't care." Sab went further: "In Christianity ... words are very important, I guess. But as you know, in Japan, especially before the Meiji (1868-1912) period, words are just words, and silence is more important."

The Trouble with Authentic Identity

Almost none of this so far has touched on the deep, inextricable, relatively ignored history of African-American music within and around bluegrass. This, in fact, almost renders most assertions of a particular kind of American authenticity in bluegrass absurd. Despite a recognition of Arnold Schultz, the African-American multi-instrumentalist, and his profound influence on the young Bill Monroe; despite the importance of African-

American musical forms throughout all American music; despite the recent prominence of artists like Rhiannon Giddens; despite no less august persons than Abigail Washburn and Bela Fleck reminding us of the Africanness of the banjo – despite all of this, the role of Southern whites in bluegrass seems to swell until it occupies most of our attention. With this kind of omission still familiar, it's hard to take definitions of "authentic American bluegrass" that deal with another national identity too seriously, when our own conception of ourselves has been so confused for so long.

In the end, maybe we're focusing too much on details like words, and missing the important silence. Maybe we're missing the lawn for the blades of bluegrass. Maybe our preoccupation with whether the Japanese are "copying," or "authentic," misses the essential journey that we're all on as we enjoy this music – from Bill Monroe's adaptation of Arnold Schultz and his Uncle Pen all the way to a young Japanese boy faithfully knocking part of the headstock off his mandolin so it looks like Bill Monroe's.

And maybe we can look forward to a time, maybe soon, when bluegrass players from Tibet, or Ghana, or Japan will excite no more comment than a banjo-picking Jewish kid from Hackensack or an African-American fiddler from Seattle. This doesn't mean that we should disregard the shades of meaning, the cultural weight, and the generations of identity that Appalachian players lovingly crafted into their music – or the American recognition and pride in a music that our big, generous, loud culture has helped to create. They're there, and that's that. But the example of Japanese bluegrass might mean that bluegrass music is big and rich enough to allow for more joyful variations, more kinds of authenticity, more flavors of genuine than we can now understand or imagine – and that's something to look forward to. ∎

Mipso joins Japanese band Bluegrass
Police onstage for an encore at Rocky Top.

SOONER OR LATER

Planted in its mountains and prairies, Oklahoma's roots music scene is on the rise

by Julie Wenger Watson

John Fullbright in his front yard, Tulsa, Oklahoma.

"[Some of these artists are] more influenced by growing up on a farm and having nothing better to do and wanting to go play piano, and then later discovering the connectedness of the things that are happening around them, which [is basically other] people that grew up on a farm and just wanted to go play piano."

Travis Linville

A GEOGRAPHICAL AND SOCIOLOGICAL crossroads, Oklahoma is both beautifully diverse and full of contradictions. The state boasts 1,600 acres of sand dunes, four mountain ranges, and 34 million acres of farmland. Once the nation's biggest oil producer and home to "Black Wall Street" – the most affluent African-American community in the US in the early 20th century – it was also the last stop on the Trail of Tears and the scene of one of the worst race riots in US history.

And always – *always* – there has been music. From the sacred sounds of the powwow drums to the twang of a country fiddle, music is as much a part of Oklahoma's history as are land runs, dust bowls, and oil barons. The roots of this state's music run deep and wide, producing everything from the socially conscious folk of Woody Guthrie and the hip-shaking rockabilly of Wanda Jackson to the Top 40 pop of Hanson and the psych-rock of the Flaming Lips. As a new crop of roots-driven Okie artists once again step into the national spotlight, the legacy continues, with a younger generation influenced in ways both subtle and overt by the history, geography, and economics of their home state.

For a state whose total population is roughly half that of the Dallas-Fort Worth metroplex, Oklahoma has sent an extraordinary number of influential musicians out into the world. A comprehensive list would fill volumes and include names like Chet Baker, Spade Cooley, Sam Rivers, Reba McEntire, Patti Page, Charlie Wilson, Garth Brooks, and Ryan Tedder. Okies Barney Kessel, Jim Keltner, Jimmy Webb, and Leon Russell were an integral part of Los Angeles' famous "Wrecking Crew," an elite group of session musicians who played on countless hit records in the 1960s and 1970s. Bob Seger and Eric Clapton loaded their bands with Oklahoma-grown talent; Tulsa native JJ Cale penned "Cocaine" – one of Clapton's biggest hits.

Jazz, blues, and country are also a huge part of Oklahoma's landscape, each playing a role in some of the state's better-known musical exports: Okemah-born folk troubadour Woody Guthrie, Leon Russell and the Tulsa Sound, and red dirt music. Although a Texan by birth, Bob Wills, the undisputed "King of Western Swing," belongs on that list, as well. From 1935 to 1942, he and his band, the Texas Playboys, broadcast their sound across the nation from Tulsa's Cain's Ballroom on radio station KVOO, popularizing this upbeat, danceable genre and making Wills an international star. The impact of these sonic heroes reverberates to this day.

The Tulsa Sound

Tulsa drummer Jamie Oldaker is a veteran of the Okie music scene, having joined the crew at Leon Russell's Shelter Records label when he was barely out of his teens. The label recorded out of a studio in a converted church near downtown Tulsa, signing artists like JJ Cale, Freddie King, the Gap Band, Phoebe Snow, Tom Petty & the Heartbreakers, and Willis Alan Ramsey. Those were heady days in Tulsa's music history – international rock stars jammed with local musicians, playing a mashup of rockabilly, country, rock, and blues that later came to be known as the Tulsa Sound, epitomized in the music of Cale and Russell.

Now 65, Oldaker has had a long and fascinating career that includes recording and touring with Clapton, Seger, Phil Collins, and many more. He's also a founding member of alt-country band the Tractors. Those are his drums you hear on Clapton's hit cover of Bob Marley's "I Shot the Sheriff."

"We went down to Miami to record it blind with a band from Tulsa," Oldaker explains. "We had no idea what we were expecting and how we were going to do it. We just listened to the song and said, 'let's do it this way,' and that's how it came out.

"Growing up here, we never copied anything," he adds. "Oklahoma musicians

don't do that. Eric Clapton told me that. He said that's what he liked about Tulsa musicians and Oklahoma musicians. They don't copy things."

Oldaker knows about stretching boundaries and breaking rules, something that continues to define the sound of a new generation of Oklahoma musicians. "We didn't have any rules," he says. "We just took [the music] and said, 'Let's play it our way.' As musicians around Tulsa back in the day, you had to be able to play country music, blues music, rock music, Motown, jazz – so we all had a chance to play different genres, and I learned different things."

Red Dirt on the Rise

With an easy grin and a laid-back manner, musician and music historian John Cooper recalls the early days of the red dirt music scene from his office in radio station KOSU above Tulsa's Woody Guthrie Center. In the early 1980s, Cooper and his buddies rented a rambling house on the edge of Stillwater, home to Oklahoma State University. Affectionately called "the Farm," it eventually became known as the birthplace of red dirt music, a genre whose own roots now extend well beyond the borders of this state, deep into Texas. In homage to the rust-tinged, iron-rich clay soil endemic in Central Oklahoma, Cooper called his band the Red Dirt Rangers.

"We were pretty isolated out there," he recalls – a sentiment echoed by countless other Okie musicians. "We had to make our own fun, and we did … with guitars and pianos and mandolins. The Farm was really the genesis spot for that sound because it was far enough outside of town where the local law enforcement didn't bother us, so the party was on."

The Farm was a musical melting pot. There, Cooper and his friends swapped licks with folks like Jimmy LaFave and Bob Childers. A young Garth Brooks was an occasional guest. Later, acts like Cross

Canadian Ragweed, Jason Boland, and Stoney LaRue joined the perpetual jam session.

As they played, a new sound emerged. Cooper describes red dirt music as the result of a couple specific influences. "I feel like there are two rivers that run into what is considered red dirt music," he says. "The first one is Bob Wills and [that spirit of] 'Let's have fun, let's party, let's forget our troubles, and let's have a great time.' The second one is Woody Guthrie – the social consciousness of 'Here's what's going on; here's what we need to fix.' I think those are the two main pillars of what is considered the red dirt scene. Let's have fun, but let's also look at what's going on. In other words, you can dance at the revolution."

A Family of Musicians

Also integral to the scene is its sense of community and support. That seems just as clear to long-time locals like Cooper as it does to newer-comers like Oklahoma City-based singer-songwriter Carter Sampson. "Oklahoma has an extraordinary amount of talent right now," Sampson says. "We have such a great community of musicians that are actually friends, that work together to create music. I'm so proud that I can call John Moreland and Travis Linville and ask them to help make me a record."

That kind of mutual support, friendship, and acceptance among Oklahoma musicians has led to a vibrant music scene, and many of its players credit this musical camaraderie as a cornerstone of their own artistic development. "People feel safe to get up and play," says Brian Horton, director of the Tulsa-based nonprofit label Horton Records. "It's very welcoming, and that's what I think fosters a lot of creativity that comes out of here, as well as a lot of freedom in music. I think that encourages integrity and authenticity in what you're doing."

L to R: Reed Mathis (Tea Leaf Green, Billy & the Kids) and John Cooper.

"The two main pillars of what is considered the red dirt scene [are:] Let's have fun, but let's also look at what's going on. In other words, you can dance at the revolution."

John Cooper

Horton points to musician Paul Benjaman's regular Sunday night residency at Tulsa venue the Colony as an example. "There are new guests every week," he says, "and different people coming to sit in – national artists popping in and getting up and playing – and it's become a really, really special thing."

John Fullbright, who recently relocated to Tulsa, has been known to show up unannounced and join in the fun. With two critically acclaimed solo albums under his belt and a third out this year, Fullbright has become somewhat of a star of the Oklahoma songwriting scene. But locals like Cooper remember him from when he was just getting started.

"The first time we saw [Fullbright] was at the Grape Ranch out there by Okemah," Cooper says. "This kid just showed up and he had a banjo. He was kind of sitting over there by himself. We went over and talked to him. [We said,] 'Hey man, do you want to play?' He sat in a little, and by about the third song in, we were like, 'Wow! This guy can play!' He tells people we were the first guys that ever got him on stage in front of people. We just felt like it was important. We could see the talent immediately. How could you miss it? He's a once-in-a-generation guy, just both his songwriting and his musicianship. The guy is phenomenal."

Cooper also recalls hearing a very young Parker Millsap. "I love Parker," he says. "I've known Parker since his mom was bringing him to a thing we have called Tuesday Night Music Club in Cushing. His mom would bring him once a month because it went late and they lived in Purcell, so it was a two-hour-plus trip."

When he's not on the road playing with Hard Working Americans or working with acts like the Secret Sisters and Elizabeth Cook, Tulsa musician Jesse Aycock can often be found at the Colony, jamming with his friends. After HWA stopped at Tulsa's Cain's Ballroom last August, Aycock treated his bandmates to an after party, Oklahoma-style. "I had Paul [Benjaman] put together an after-party at the Colony," Aycock remembers. "I dragged half of the band there, and we all ended up playing, of course, and we all got to hear everyone else play because Paul invited all the other friends out."

What Makes the Oklahoma Sound

Aycock believes it's cross-pollination from these wide-open jams that makes the music from Oklahoma so special. "The music that's coming out of here influences me a ton," he says. "A lot of it is with current artists who are my friends, that I'm around and that I play with or just listen to. [John] Moreland is one of those and Paul [Benjaman] and Dustin [Pittsley]. … It's all a building block in the way that you play, in the way that you communicate musically. It's all just a language. I think it's something that's continued from the early days here, and Bob Wills was even doing this, going over to North Tulsa after hours and playing with the jazz players and developing his sound.

"There's been so many times where you've got jazz drummers that come out of the jazz world playing with a country artist," he continues. "Or you've got a blues artist playing with a folk artist, and everyone is coming from these different

areas and then playing together and trying to really play to the song and to learn each other's styles."

It's possible the actual geography of the state contributes to this genre-hopping, musical fluidity inherent in the Oklahoma sound. Singer-songwriter Travis Linville – Hayes Carll's go-to guitarist who also produced Sampson's new album *Wilder Side* – grew up in Chickasha, in South-Central Oklahoma. "You could say that halfway in the middle of Oklahoma is this geological situation that turns from what is the Eastern United States into what is the plains," he says. "This flat, open territory that maybe belonged to the Comanche is sort of like being out in the ocean. So the eastern half of this state is this one thing, and then the western half is practically the introduction to the desert. There's a certain amount of openness and an amount of emptiness out there that I think inspires art. Maybe there's something about the introduction to the plains and the idea of very rural country and then a little urban spot in there like Tulsa or Oklahoma City. The urban spots in extremely rural areas have a uniqueness about them."

While Linville can pinpoint his influences as Oklahoma musicians like Woody Guthrie, JJ Cale, and Leon Russell, he also recognizes that his home state itself plays a role. "I think it's more possible we're all influenced by the same things – the same culture, and the same whatever-it-is that makes Oklahoma. What is it? I don't know," he laughs. "If you asked some of these artists about the artists they're seemingly influenced by, you'd probably find out that really, they're more influenced by growing up on a

> **"[In Oklahoma,] you don't have to work a job so hard that you don't have anything left at the end of the day. You can afford to do things here. You can even go out and experience music and get inspired a lot more during the week because you're not just completely exhausted."**
>
> Jesse Aycock

farm and having nothing better to do and wanting to go play piano and then later discovering the connectedness of the things that are happening around them, which [is basically other] people that grew up on a farm and just wanted to go play piano."

With his own roots in small-town Oklahoma, Paul Benjaman may well agree. Quick to laugh and with an affable grin and a mane of unruly curls, Benjaman's charming accent reveals his rural childhood. "I was just a little kid living out in Inola," he says of his musical beginnings. "The very first record I had when I was a kid was a hand-me-down copy of Sly and the Family Stone's greatest hits. So here's this little kid out on a ten-acre farm, and you know he doesn't see other kids all day. He was the first child, and he's got this little record player with Sly and the Family Stone's greatest hits, and he's listening to it all day. There's no real peer influence." He laughs. "I was really into *Star Wars*, and I was really into Sly and the Family Stone.

"My dad had Stevie Wonder on some 8-tracks, and he also had John Denver, and we would put one in after the other," he continues. "When you're a kid, that's the cool thing. You can approach it from that innocence. You don't even know the concept of a scene or something like that, so pretty much Stevie Wonder and John Denver, they're the same person to you. You can see them both on TV and one's with the Muppets. You don't get into

processing it. It's all sound. It all kind of crosses over."

Roots rocker JD McPherson recently moved to Nashville and tours the world these days, but, much like Benjaman and Linville, he spent his early years in the Oklahoma countryside. "It just really seemed like a cocoon," he says. "When I was growing up and learning to play guitar and getting into music, it was really that way because I grew up in Southeast Oklahoma, where there's absolutely nothing except time to listen to music and practice every day."

McPherson eventually moved to Norman, to attend the University of Oklahoma. "When I was actually playing shows every weekend, it was with four Oklahoma musicians," he says, "and I was going to see Oklahoma bands a lot. It seemed like it was a little culture in the most accurate description of a culture, in that it sort of stays separate from other things. People like Travis Linville, Mike Hosty, Brian Parton – all of these people around here were really influential for me."

For better or worse, Oklahoma is a relatively inexpensive place to live, too. While some like to think it's the supportive community, the fabulous clubs and venues, and the rich history that contribute to the creation of so many quality musicians, cheap rent may be an equally important factor. "Sometimes it's purely economic," suggests Grammy Museum Executive Director Bob Santelli. "I have studies of, let's just call them

scenes, in cities and almost always it starts with affordable living and places for musicians to play."

The musicians themselves tend to put it more bluntly. "It's so stinkin' cheap to live here," says singer-songwriter Samantha Crain. John Moreland echoes that when asked what keeps him in the state. "Cheap rent," he says, and Carter Sampson joins the chorus: "It's a totally affordable place to live, which allows me to tour a lot."

Jesse Aycock explains further. "[The low cost of living] is great because it allows you the freedom of creating. You don't have to work a job so hard that you don't have anything left at the end of the day. You can afford to do things here. You can even go out and experience music and get inspired a lot more during the week because you're not just completely exhausted."

Brian Horton concurs. "A lot of artists here, over the years they've been comfortable with making a living. As long as they're not starving and can play music for a living and provide just the basic things, in a lot of ways they're happy and they've found that balance."

While the cheap rent, camaraderie, and mutual support might keep some musicians in the state, its conservative politics can have the opposite effect. Brian Haas, founding member and keyboardist for the progressive jazz band Jacob Fred Jazz Odyssey, is an Okie who now resides in New Mexico. "I don't know why so may Oklahoma musicians choose

Jesse Aycock (Hard Working Americans)
outside Cain's Ballroom, Tulsa, Oklahoma.

"I am connected to Oklahoma because I'm an Oklahoman, and it will forever be an influence to my writing, but it has always been, and most likely will always be, a clashing love/hate relationship."

Samantha Crain

to keep a home in Oklahoma," he says. "It must be the progressive politics, natural gas oligarchs, school funding, injection-well-created earthquakes, racist cops, Confederate flag bumper stickers placed near scrotal balls hanging from the backs of pickups, and the oil refineries within the city limits for all to breathe," he jokes. "But when I did live in Oklahoma, the things I enjoyed most were the national forests, state parks, abundant waterways, and friendly people."

Crain, who is of Choctaw heritage and grew up in the town of Shawnee, also struggles to reconcile these apparent contradictions. "You have to understand that the whole reason I wanted to play music and tour was because I was sick of Oklahoma," she says. "I was more or less an outcast, too far off-center for these small towns. I didn't fit in; I still don't. It's taken me a long time to come around to wanting to find the good in this place – and the good definitely exists. I had to go away to come back, I guess.

"Most of my sense of Oklahoma that comes through in my writing is

very conflicted," she adds, "as is my relationship with this community of people. I see the general kindness, but I also see the hatred that deep, institutionalized fear brings against so many people. I see the beauty of the Wichita Mountains and the Tallgrass Prairie, but I also see the ugliness that years of greed have carved into the ground here. I see the greatness of inspiring people like [ballerina] Maria Tallchief and [humorist] Will Rogers, but I also see how the Indian population of this state has been disregarded and forgotten. I am connected to Oklahoma because I'm an Oklahoman, and it will forever be an influence to my writing, but it has always been, and most likely will always be, a clashing love/hate relationship."

That ambivalence, those contra-dictions, is, perhaps, part of what it means to be an Oklahoma musician. Beauty, diversity, and petroleum profits juxtaposed with violence, poverty, and intolerance. Reconciling this Okie paradox was, arguably, a driving

force behind the music of troubadour and activist Woody Guthrie, whose own relationship with his home state was a complicated one. Often a source of frustration, the state and its incongruities are also a wellspring of creativity, inspiring truly outstanding music as artists attempt to make sense of the world around them.

While it's clear no one factor is responsible for Oklahoma's steady production of musical talent, it's equally apparent that the state – through its history, culture, and even geographic diversity – once again has a hand in inspiring a whole new wave of gifted musicians. As for the luck that has placed all these great new artists in the same generation, Aycock muses: "It's timing. … It's just the cycle of things, and it all falls into place how it should. It seems like when one thing falls into place, there's something that follows behind it, and it's all supposed to play out that way. And right now, it seems like it's the right time for these artists to really push into bigger things." ■

Parker Millsap.

THE YODELIN' OUTLAW

Tommy Ash rises out of Phoenix

by Gwendolyn Elliott

"[Yodeling is] definitely not sexy, but it's got its roots."

Tommy Ash

I ALWAYS GET, 'WHICH ONE OF YOU is Tommy?'" says Phoenix, Arizona-based singer-songwriter Tommy Ash. "And I'm like, 'That's me.' [Then] they'll say, 'You're a lot better looking than I thought you'd be.'"

Indeed, Ash looks more like a runway model than the DIY outlaw country singer she is. Her desert-bleached mane and winsome smile call to mind Christie Brinkley in a cowboy hat, threatening to overshadow her talent if you don't pause to listen. And her pitch-perfect voice, with just a hint of gravel, sounds easy and natural, not as though it's been honed over years of performing. No question the 28-year-old singer has natural ability in spades, but Ash has been refining her act from a very young age.

Her voice teacher, she says, "was an opera singer. She had me bring in songs [I wanted to sing], and I brought in these country songs. When [I sang for her], she tried to make me sing it a little too clean, and too perfect, and that's what I didn't like; I liked the grit. In a lot of those old country songs, you didn't hear perfection, you heard those little flaws. It was good ear training, learning how to breathe and just tightening up little things here and there; but opera and country, it just doesn't mix."

Further back, when she was around five years old, Ash began to round the local talent show circuit, singing in Phoenix-area honky-tonks like the now-shuttered Mr. Lucky's and Graham Central Station, chaperoned by her parents. The first time she heard LeAnn Rimes on the radio, when she was about 10 years old, she took up yodeling. "I was like, 'Yeah, this is it,'" she says. "She covered a lot of older artists, she did an album with some Patsy Cline songs, some Waylon Jennings, and I started listening to her influences more and more."

A New Kind of Outlaw

These days, her interest – and ability – in yodeling is a small but integral part of her style. "I don't do it as much anymore," she says. "It's not as cute as it was when I was younger."

But the rootsy twang it adds to a song like "Yodelin' Blues," a haunting, dust-caked country ballad from her 2013 debut *Sinner's Blood*, is undeniable. As much as it nods to the troubadour tradition of Jimmie Rodgers, it's perfect for the honky-tonk sound Ash is making today, even if so few artists are doing it. "It's definitely not sexy," she says, "but it's got its roots."

Yodeling also happens to be really hard, for the untrained, to pull off in a way that sounds genuine, and the pure sound of Country Music Hall of Famer Patsy Montana comes up. Ash cites Montana as one of the first female outlaws. "She's singing 'Cowboy's Sweetheart,' she's yodeling, she's saying she wants to rope and ride like the boys, and kind of rough it out," she says.

Montana and others like her, Ash adds, "paved the way for women outlaws. That's what Ameripolitan is, what Americana is. It's the artist that has just created their own sound and I think that's what's so outlaw about it, that we're just doing our own thing, we're not following the mold of what country is or should be. We're just *roots*."

Ash's musings sync up with her reputation in the indie country scene. She is regularly lauded on the music blog We Hate Pop Country!, recently as one of "5 Females in Country Music that You Just Need to Know About." With her Tommy Ash Band, local alt-weekly *Phoenix New-Times* has tuned in too, awarding her multiple nods in the paper's 2015 Best Of issue, including one for "Best Local Country Band." Most recently, she was nominated for a 2016 Ameripolitan Music Award for Best Female Outlaw.

To boot, a quick stroll through Ash's online trove of videos and songs shows how aligned the singer is with the outlaw ethos. *Sinner's Blood* features eight Ash-penned songs about lost love ("Yodelin' Blues"), raucous, righteous anthems ("Sinner's Blood"), and lusty laments ("Cowboys Gone"). In their live shows, she and her band often cover classic Waylon, Willie, and Cash. With a woman behind the mic singing, "The Only *Mama* That'll Walk the Line," it's a nod to Linda Ronstadt and Ash's hero LeAnn Rimes, and one nicely tailored to Ash herself, as Jennings spent some of his early years in Phoenix.

"I'm influenced by everything, not just Waylon Jennings," she says. "Obviously he's the outlaw man, and I love the heavy kick drum, [and the] grungier sound of his music, how it feels so real. And his voice, it's not perfect, there's cracks and little flaws. I love the sounds of Buck Owens [too] – anything that's a traditional sound. I love shuffles and train beats. I love the high singing voice of Patsy Cline. Dwight Yoakam has so many sounds and flavors to his music, he has the rock vibe, he has the traditional country – it's just a blend of everything."

Yoakam, a fellow yodeler, even hired Ash and her band to open for him at the Phoenix stop on his 3 Pears tour. The appearance added to a growing roster

of nationally touring, outlaw-tinged acts that are keen to share a bill with the troupe, including Dale Watson, Merle Haggard, Billy Bob Thornton and the Boxmasters, Ryan Bingham, and others.

Yet the Phoenix country scene on the whole, Ash says – once choked with authentic honky-tonks and divey watering holes doubling as music venues – "is slowly dying. The Toby Keiths and the Dierks Bentleys, they're taking over pretty much all the clubs. Today's music is taking over; all the little bars are pretty much gone and shut down." Of course, Keith's recently opened I Love This Bar and Grill has now closed, but Phoenix native Bentley's live music venue Whiskey Row is still in operation.

No Thanks to Nashville

Even as the pop- and alt-country worlds continue to drift apart, artists like Tommy Ash continue to buck the trends. The singer is in good company among Margo Price, Bonnie Montgomery, Lera Lynn, Jesse Lafser, Sarah Gayle Meech, Lydia Loveless, Darci Carlson, Rachel Brooke, and Nikki Lane (a friend of Ash's). They're a new wave of women in outlaw country not seen since the likes of Jesse Coulter and Loretta Lynn, and arguably never in such numbers. This is notwithstanding the excellent contributions of folks like Sturgill Simpson, Whitey Morgan, Dale Watson, and Chris Stapleton – arguably outlaw's new Highwaymen.

"I have talked to a few producers," she says. "I went out to meet them in Nashville and they listened to my songs and thought they were great. But they also wanted to push me in a more 'sweet American girl' [direction], and they had this vision of what they wanted me to be, and they were telling me how they were going to hire someone to create this look for me.

"I was like, 'Whoa, whoa. Wait a minute. First off, I have my own look, I'm not just going to take any look,'" she says. "They loved my voice, but I'm like, 'I'm not just a good voice, I've got great songs here, too, you know.' At the end they're like, 'We need this money and we're going to make this happen for you, we're going to create you.' I'm like, 'Well, shit, if I'm going to give you my money I might as well keep it myself and be myself. I don't need to pay you to create me, I'm already here!'"

Ash says she'll channel some of that spitfire into her new album, which at the time of this writing was getting started at the Fivethirteen recording studio in Phoenix.

Her first time in the studio, she says, "was a really stressful process, and we did it all on our own. We had no money, we were working full-time jobs, we would go gig at night almost every single night, and the nights we had off, we'd go to work and get to the studio and try to finish."

Now, Ash says, "[I'm] a little more clear of who I am, and the art of what I'm doing." ■

ALL OR NOTHIN'

Nikki Lane follows her own road *by Joshua M. Miller*

ONE OF THE FIRST THINGS YOU notice about Nikki Lane is that she's constantly on the move. It's fitting: Lane's story stretches across immense lengths of highway, through towns both big and small. She grew up in Greenville, South Carolina, but got out the first chance she could. For the next decade or so, she spent time living in Los Angeles and New York before settling in Nashville.

In 2011, Lane released her debut album, *Walk of Shame*. Three years later, she followed it with *All or Nothin'*, produced by the Black Keys' Dan Auerbach. She spent 18 months touring the album, first opening and then headlining shows. A new effort due this fall, at press time tentatively titled *Highway Queen*, was recorded at the famed Electric Lady Studios in New York.

Through it all, Lane feels her ability to adapt to new surroundings has aided her pursuits. "All the places I've lived taught me to be flexible with everything," she says. "I've learned to be comfortable wherever I am. Each time, the adjustment phase got shorter. It made me more creative because I didn't have the crutch of familiarity. Moving around has forced me to get comfortable quick."

Fellow musician Butch Walker, with whom Lane has toured, agrees. "She's not afraid to get dirt under her fingernails and go anywhere and sleep in a sleeping bag and put in the hours," he says. "I think it builds character that's not there if you spend all your time in your hometown and never get out and see the rest of the world."

Indeed, Lane has learned to fend for herself, and her songs reflect that fearless nature and independence. Her music is often described as outlaw country – a description she thinks fits, as she's going against the grain of much of today's radio-friendly pop country.

"I think being yourself and hoping they'll accept you is way less stressful than playing a part and hoping people will buy it," she says. "There are repercussions to having a big mouth and putting my foot down about certain things, but I would say it balances out with rewards because people notice it and *you* notice it. I'd rather be known for speaking the truth – even if it's just *my* truth – than playing a part."

Growing Up Tough

Lane's parents divorced early on, and she and her younger sister began splitting time between her mother, who valued properness, and her father, who raced professional motocross.

"I grew up with a single mother, and visiting this wild-ass redneck on the weekend," she says. "It's an interesting way to grow up. I grew up trying to be a Southern lady five days of the week and then going out to the country ... and [being] allowed to cuss over the weekends. It made both my sister and I pretty balanced."

Though music wasn't a big part of her upbringing, Lane's father mostly listened to '80s country and her mother listened to Motown. Her own music tastes were limited largely by what she heard on the radio. "I didn't have a very well-versed

taste in music until I got out of my hometown," she says.

She dropped out of high school at 17 and thought she might move to California to be a fashion designer. "I was trying to be defiant," she says. "I didn't have a great plan, I just wanted to get out."

When she told her parents of her plan, hoping that their resistance would make her defiance even sweeter, she was surprised to find they were very supportive. "That shocked me," she recalls, "because I didn't picture my parents as the kind of people who would push me to do something. I pictured them as people that would tell me not to do something."

So with no resistance to her escape plan, Lane finally set out for Los Angeles two years later, in early 2003. During almost five years in the City of Angels, her eyes opened to the wider world around her. She discovered artists she wasn't familiar with, who became major influences.

"I remember someone giving me mushrooms and putting on Neil Young's *After the Gold Rush*, and it blowing my mind," she says. "I was like 'Who is this guy? And – what? There's 15 more of these records?'"

Still, her interest in fashion continued, and she decided to start a shoe company, which she called Nikki Lane – a nickname her friends came up with while they were watching *Almost Famous*. The name stuck and she took it as her own.

Still, she began to feel that L.A. had given her all it could. "I had dug into every nook and cranny of L.A.," she says, "and I knew what I wanted from there, so I was like 'What's next?' New York. I had to give it a try."

With that decision made, four weeks before her move, she began performing her own music. It started out as a joke – she wrote melodies while she sat in traffic. But one of her friends commented that she should try performing, so she played a couple shows, including her going-away party, and the seed was planted.

Shifting Gears in New York

When she arrived in New York at the end of 2007, she decided she needed to update her identity to fit with her

new corporate job handling design development and denim with Mark Ecko. Then came a marriage to singer-songwriter Joseph Plunkett (Joseph Plunkett & the Weight) in August 2009.

"I had a specific look [in L.A.]," she says, "and when I moved to New York, I was convinced I had to become this other character. I sold all my clothes and took a job in the city. ... Within four months I was trying to buy all my dresses back from my friends. I moved over to Williamsburg [in Brooklyn]. ... I was able to be comfortable there and figure out things like music. I didn't need to work in a corporate job and have that success level to look the way that I thought I did."

Butch Walker says he first met Lane at What Goes Around Comes Around, a high-fashion secondhand clothing store she managed near Greenwich Village after leaving her gig in the fashion industry. They talked a little bit about their taste in country music and Lane invited him to see her perform at a bar where she was also the bartender. "At the end of the night," he remembers, "I put my guitar in her hand and she sat up on the bar, fearless. Everyone got really quiet, and she sang a couple of her own songs and really blew me away. I was like, 'Wait a minute, why aren't you doing this for a living?'"

For a while, it seemed like music was merely a hobby. But her passion for it grew thanks to a community of supportive musicians. Among them were Kevn Kinney from Drivin' N' Cryin' and his wife, Shayni Rae. Lane first met them at the now-defunct National Underground, which hosted events featuring folk and country artists. While Lane couldn't play many chords on guitar at the time, Rae saw something special in her music and convinced her to keep performing. That and Lane's abrupt divorce from Plunkett pushed her over the edge as a songwriter. Her angst and inspiration began pouring out in the form of songs.

"That's really where music came in full force for me, because it was go time," Lane says. "I wouldn't have written those songs if I wasn't down on my ass in a town for a minute." With encouragement and confidence, Lane decided it was time to commit to music full-time, record an album (*Walk of Shame*), and move to Nashville.

> "There are repercussions to having a big mouth and putting my foot down about certain things, but … I'd rather be known for speaking the truth – even if it's just *my* truth – than playing a part."
>
> Nikki Lane

"I set myself up in New York that there was no turning back," she says. "[But then] New York gave me the courage to say, 'I don't need to be up here working 70 hours a week.' … I want to go down there to Nashville to make a country record, and come back here and have a car service drive me around."

All or Nothing in Nashville

Once in Nashville, she began discovering that Music City's music community was one of the most tight-knit she'd been part of. Kinney and his wife helped introduce her around.

"They're a big part of my career because when I said I was moving to Nashville, they knew everyone down there," says Lane. "[Shayni] paid for her own plane ticket and flew to Nashville with me, and introduced me to every single person that I worked with the next five years."

Among those she met during her early days in Nashville were fellow transplants like Jonny Fritz, Langhorne Slim, and JD McPherson. "They're the only people I can call and talk to about my insecurities growing in this business," Lane says. "[Nashville's] got a lot of key players that have kept me doing this job when I might have otherwise thrown in the towel. They reminded me this was the [same] struggle for everyone."

One day, Lane was buying and selling items at a flea market and Black Keys frontman Dan Auerbach asked if she wanted to trade her '40s trapper jacket for something. She didn't know who he was at the time and passed, opting for cash payment.

Soon after, she was hired to be an assistant for a *GQ* cover shoot, which turned out to be focused on the Black Keys. Again, she talked briefly with Auerbach. When her single from her debut came out two weeks later, she received a text from him: "You didn't tell me you played music, this track is awesome." Without hesitation she texted him back: "Cool, you'll make my next record." And a couple months later they were in the studio. It was a bold move, to be sure, but Lane doesn't hesitate to explain: "You have to throw it out there."

She felt very comfortable working with Auerbach, and the sessions went so well that a chance get-together between Auerbach's father, Chuck, and his backyard neighbor Buddy Miller over coffee opened the door to Lane's label, New West Records, after she'd spent a year looking for someone to release the disc.

"Dan's father, Chuck, had coffee with Buddy, and he was like, 'You should get Nikki a record deal,'" she says. "All the pull in world didn't get me a record deal, but one man walking across the street and having a cup of coffee with Buddy Miller got me a record deal."

The Road Ahead

With those kinds of connections and her tough nature, the future looks bright for Lane as she preps the release of *Highway Queen*. In what she describes as an "experimental phase," she recorded 11 tracks with producer Jonathan Wilson at Electric Lady Studios in New York, where her manager Lee Foster oversees operations. Lane realized she had a stronger opinion on production this time than she previously did, but admits she feels nervous about what people expect from her sound.

"[*Highway Queen*] has to stand up to the last record but also carry me further than the last record, because I have to grow off that foundation," she says. "I want to keep getting better and make sure I love what we make. … I'm still trying to define what's it's going to be like, which is why [the release] keeps getting pushed back."

As for the album's material, Lane's recent touring inspired many of the lyrics. "There's a lot of talking about driving around in a van," she says, "which is why I want to call it *Highway Queen*."

And she thrives on live shows, "It's like clockwork. I go out and do my job," Lane says. "There's no insecurity because I've done it every day. If you do something 300 times, you better figure that shit out or quit."

Besides, she adds, "Touring has allowed me to make friends out of fans. They hang out with me and cook me dinner and I know their kid's name. These people are the reason you get to do your job. … The more work I put into [music and touring], the more gratification I have on a personal level." ∎

North American Busk

PHOTOGRAPHS
BY JASON GOODMAN

Street musicians cut through the noise. They demand attention. It's not enough to be odd or entertaining. We pedestrians have places to go and things to do. We want something we've never seen or heard before. Something to hook us beyond a vague passing curiosity. Something to make us stop and listen before we even realize we've chosen to do so. Whether it's on a subway platform in New York or a town square in South Florida, the Arizona desert or downtown Boston, the street musician's job is to reach into the air and find the music we all have in common – no matter who we are or where we're headed. We may never know their name or hear their song again, but for a moment, one otherwise busy day, they got us to stop and listen to strangers, among strangers.

Mallory Square just after sunset.
Key West, Florida / 2007

Brooklyn-bound L Train stop.
New York City / 2006

Moe Pope behind 337 Summer Street.
Boston, Massachusetts / 2006

Pianist in DUMB
Brooklyn, New York / 20

One-man band at Honk Fest.
Cambridge, Massachusetts / 2006

He lost his leg hopping trains out West.
Portland, Maine / 2014

Somewhere in
Northwest Arizona / 2012

DAWG DNA

**David Grisman
and half a century
of unabashedly
acoustic music**

by Kent Gustavson

"Ralph Rinzler called me up, and he said, 'I'm going down to Rising Sun, Maryland, to hear Bill Monroe, do you want to come?' And you know, I didn't need a second invitation. And that changed my life, you know. That changed my life."

David Grisman

DAVID "DAWG" GRISMAN HAS fiercely defended the resonating bodies of acoustic instruments for half a century. His great advocacy for acoustic music even brought friend and legendary rocker Jerry Garcia of the Grateful Dead to record folk songs at Grisman's home in the early 1990s (immortalized by the intimate documentary *Grateful Dawg*).

Grisman lightheartedly speaks of only two major breaches of his acoustic-only career. Once, he lost a battle with the elder statesman of European string jazz, Danish fiddler Svend Asmussen (who turned 100 years old in February), who insisted on plugging in his electric violin on their 1987 record *Svingin' with Svend*. And during his experimental early years, Grisman performed on an electric mandocello with his psychedelic rock band Earth Opera. The remainder of his half-century career has been devoted to tunes that spin and spit from the wood and steel of acoustic instruments.

Grisman compares his love of acoustic music to a well-crafted fiddle. "Somebody built this violin 200 years ago," he says, "and it was a real piece of wood. It was a real tree. There's nothing attached to it but somebody's hands, and it allows their personality to come through, as well as the personality of the instrument. It's almost a prerequisite for real music."

When questioned about "real music," and his dogged stick-to-your-guns averseness to "innovations" involving electronic musical instruments, pick-up systems, and amplification, Grisman laughs: "I have to say it. I may be going down with the ship, but it's true. Believe me, a lot of guys have come to me with pick-ups and instruments; there's a reason I never picked up on any of it. Because it just didn't sound as good."

As earthy and simple as Grisman's music has sounded throughout the four decades his own quintet (now a sextet) has been active, it is also informed by strains of gypsy music, jazz, world music, classical, rock, pop, and bluegrass. Grisman's albums and projects are always Velveteen Rabbit-real, and no matter whether a melody is a new original, an old standard, or a traditional tune, Grisman's arrangements and deft performances digest notes and regurgitate a new, shiny sound that shouts all kinds of primary and secondary colors, sometimes Coltrane, sometimes Monroe.

While Old and in the Way – his groundbreaking 1973 bluegrass project with Jerry Garcia, Peter Rowan, Vassar Clements, John Kahn, Richard Greene, and John Hartford – was touring, Garcia christened Grisman with the nickname "Dawg," and in January 1976, when Grisman performed his first gig with the David Grisman Quintet, the name "Dawg music" stuck. Four decades later, Dawg music is here to stay.

Just as sweet treble stylings spill out of the f-holes of his ancient-toned mandolin, Grisman fingers note-paths across his fretboard and carves concert tours through the backroads of the country with great joy and fervor. After thousands of appearances, countless records, and and stages shared with countless greats – from Doc Watson to the Grateful Dead – Grisman is still touring at age 70, and loving it.

Of touring, Grisman says, with palpable excitement, "I feel like I've still got something to contribute. And there's nobody else that's doing it quite like I do. ... I'm trying! I think I'm still louder than Chris Thile." Then, under his breath, he adds, "Unless he plugs in, man."

The Artistic Side

In 1947, at age two, David Grisman was brought by his mother, Fanya, to her middle school classroom in Passaic, New Jersey, where she taught art to an excited group of students, including Ralph Rinzler, who was then 12 years old. Toddler David didn't remember their first meeting, but years later, his friend Rinzler recounted the experience to him. Fourteen years after first crossing paths with Grisman, Rinzler became known for bringing Doc Watson into the public eye and managing both Watson and Bill Monroe through much of the 1960s.

Grisman grew up in a conservative Jewish household and, like many children, started learning to play the piano during elementary school. He had a fairly normal childhood, but then he lost his father at age ten, and as he recalls, "I had a tough time with my mom; she was kind of overbearing a little bit, for me." He turned to music as an

outlet. At first, he listened to the same things that other kids did, like Frankie Lymon and the Teenagers, Chuck Berry, and Buddy Holly, until he heard the call of something different: The Kingston Trio, with their big hit "Tom Dooley" in 1958.

Then, Grisman remembers, "When I was 15, and developing an interest in folk music, I asked my favorite high school teacher, Elsie Rinzler, to help form a folk music club." She agreed and soon invited her cousin Ralph to her English classroom at Passaic Junior High School. Grisman and his two friends, Fred Weisz and Jack Scott, were amazed by this "professional" folk musician, with his guitar, banjo, and mandolin and his "dissertation and demonstration of folk music." With a twinkle in his eye, Grisman recalls, "Hearing him speak about folk music, sing, and play guitar, banjo, and mandolin that day obviously changed my life." Rinzler soon became a "guru in many things, musical and otherwise."

Grisman remembers clearly how drawn he was to folk music in his teenage years, after the seeming collapse of rock and roll. "In the '50s," he says, "the rock and roll explosion happened, and we were all caught up with that, but it kind of evaporated in the end of the '50s, you know. Elvis went into the army. Buddy Holly got killed. Frankie Lyman OD'd. Chuck Berry went to jail. Jerry Lee Lewis got caught in a scandal. Little Richard found the Lord. It all evaporated around 1960. But there was the Kingston Trio, and for me, that was the birth of the folk movement."

Today, Grisman draws an even deeper connection between his beginnings in folk music and his late friend Ralph Rinzler. "Years later, in 1990, when Ralph visited me in California, he revealed that it had been my mother who 'opened up' the artistic, aesthetic side of his nature, by the way she taught art. He couldn't paint or draw, but the way she taught art turned a screw in his head. The thing is, I was never able to get that from my mom. I got it from Ralph

instead. And so I received a gift from my mom through Ralph.

"I learned so much from him," Grisman adds. "He took us under his wing, and we would go over to his place. He lived two blocks away from me, and one block away from one of the other guys. At the time, right around 1961, Ralph was working for British Overseas Airline Company. He'd come home from work late, and we'd go over there at around 10:30 at night. He turned us on to all kinds of music, playing tapes and playing music with us. At midnight, without fail, the phone would ring. It would wake up Ralph's dad, who was a doctor, and he would get mad, and I'd have to go home."

The boys' drive to learn was not easily satiated, and Grisman and his friends "all started getting interested in the real stuff." Grisman recalls, "We might have heard the Kingston Trio first, but it wasn't too long before we heard – and were digging – Mississippi John Hurt, Skip James, and people like the New Lost City Ramblers. We could go hear this music, and it was amazing. All these kindred spirits, all these young kids like me, were gathered in the same places, interested in various aspects of American roots music."

Rinzler was a powerful force in Grisman's life for all of his teenage years. One highlight was the day when Rinzler returned from a trip to Shouns, Tennessee, with a tape that he played for 15-year-old Grisman. "He was really excited about having rediscovered Clarence Ashley, who had made records in the '20s, you know," Grisman says. "I was sitting there listening, saying, 'Who's that playing the guitar?'" It was Rinzler's first recording of Arthel "Doc" Watson, who was playing rhythm and lead guitar for Clarence "Tom" Ashley's small ensemble at the time. When Watson later visited New York City, Rinzler gave Grisman the all-important job of guide, and Grisman remembers spending hours with Doc.

Most importantly for the young mandolin player, Grisman recalls one

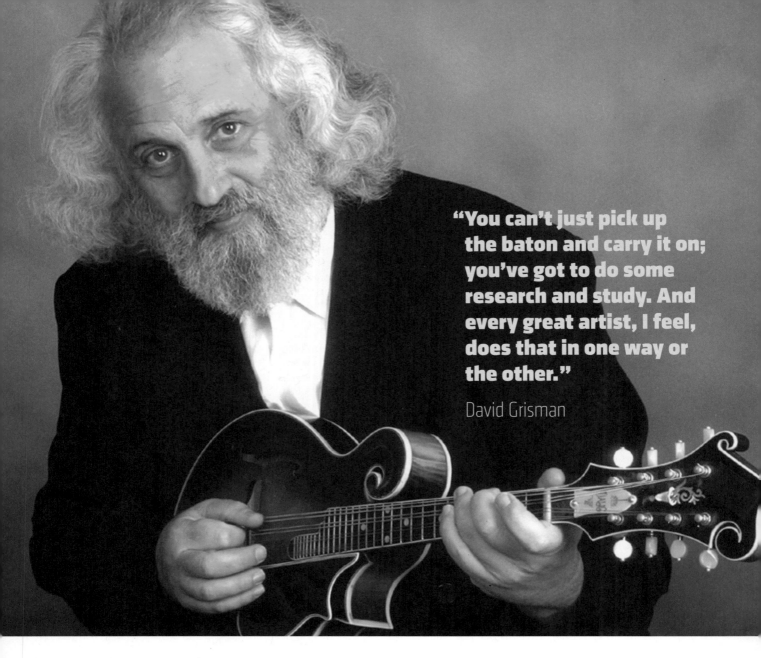

> "You can't just pick up the baton and carry it on; you've got to do some research and study. And every great artist, I feel, does that in one way or the other."
>
> David Grisman

morning in 1961 when the phone rang at his mother's house. "Ralph Rinzler called me up, and he said, 'I'm going down to Rising Sun, Maryland, to hear Bill Monroe, do you want to come?' And you know, I didn't need a second invitation. And that changed my life, you know. That changed my life."

The Youngest Guy in the Band

While still in high school, David Grisman and his friends Fred and Jack discovered what they called "The Square" on Sunday afternoons. The fountain in Washington Square Park, in Greenwich Village, had played host since the late 1940s to an incredibly diverse collection of folk musicians. "They had all these musicians gathered around the fountain," Grisman remembers. "There would be old-time musicians, ragtime fingerpickers, political protest singers, bluegrass guys, blues guys, and old Italian guys sitting there playing chess."

Maria Muldaur, then a teenager, also frequented the Square. "In 1962," she recalls, "I ran into a young mandolin player in Washington Square Park one day named David Grisman. His mom was still bringing him from New Jersey to the Park to play, and we formed a group called Maria and the Washington Square Ramblers. We actually got a little gig every Sunday at a funny Italian restaurant on Long Island whose owners had decided that folk music was the new biggest thing, and they wanted to present what they called 'folk music' to draw people into the restaurant. Wow! Our first paying gig!"

Later the same year, Grisman remembers, "Doc Watson was the first professional musician to ever invite me onto stage. It was during one of Doc's early engagements at Gerde's Folk City, and I think Ralph's younger cousin Richard put a bug in Doc's ear about me having a mandolin with me. In any case, he invited me up on stage to play a song or two. I remember playing 'In the Pines' and perhaps another tune. It made a profound impact on me."

That year, Grisman also started attending NYU, and spent all of the time he could outside of class playing music. He also got a job working at Israel "Izzy" Young's Folklore Center, which was arguably the most important hangout for folk musicians in New York at the time. Grisman remembers, "Bob Dylan was sleeping on Israel Young's floor sometimes. And I used to sell things, like one guitar string to Richie Havens, who would run in there in between sets, and had been playing on five strings. It was a great time."

During his second year of college, he rented a little walk-up apartment for $58, at 80 Thompson Street. "It had DC current and a bathtub in the kitchen," Grisman remembers, but his memories are nothing but fond. "It was just a wonderful time, a wonderful place, and I met a lot of people that I am still friends with."

Grisman started to form a group of peers who were all talented musicians, and they began to explore various genres together. "David Lindley, Ry Cooder, Jerry Garcia, and others," he says, "we were all around the same age. Some were a little older, and some were a little younger, but we were all World War II babies." He also connected with what they called the "older generation" that his mentor and friend Ralph Rinzler belonged to. "Mike Seeger, John Cohen, and those guys were kind of the older generation of folk musicians. Some of these guys, as years went on, became more like peers and friends. But, back then, we were young kids to them."

Alongside his classes at NYU, Grisman started to study music very seriously. "You have to study," he says.

"For something to come out, you have to take a lot in. And it's got to be the correct stuff." He worked hard on his instrument of choice, and he went as far as he could to the source of the music, with the help of Rinzler and other new friends in the folk music scene. He soon had a chance to sit and study with some of his heroes, but he started with recordings. "I hung out with Frank Wakefield, the great mandolin player, and he showed me a whole bunch of Bill Monroe solos that he'd learned, note-for-note, by slowing down records, and showed me that that's what was necessary. And I learned those Bill Monroe solos."

It didn't take long until Grisman started passing the knowledge he had gained along to others, as he has now done time after time, over his half-century-long career. "When a 14-year-old Andy Statman came to me for his first mandolin lesson, I saw he had great talent, and I said, 'Here are a bunch of tapes. Learn the stuff that's on these tapes!'

"If you're going to learn an instrument," he adds, "you've got to learn what's been done on that instrument, at least in a certain area." His own explorations went beyond one area, and he notes that even at the beginning of his career, "I tried to incorporate a lot of areas; I tried to do a thorough study of bluegrass mandolin playing in the 1960s, of my heroes, Bill Monroe, Bobby Osborne, Jesse McReynolds, and Frank Wakefield. You can't just pick up the baton and carry it on; you've got to do some research and study. And every great artist, I feel, does that in one way or the other. I think it's a necessary process to prime your own voice.

"It's been a lifetime of listening, really," he adds. "It's all about processing every-thing you are taking in, drawing on all these influences, whether you are figuring out what Bill Monroe played, what Jesse McReynolds played, learning a Billy Strayhorn tune, a Django Reinhardt tune, learning a Django Reinhardt tune from Stephane Grappelli, learning a Django Reinhardt tune from Svend

Asmussen, or whatever other situation you find yourself in."

On a Sunday afternoon in the summer of 1964, Grisman first met Jerry Garcia in West Grove, Pennsylvania, where they were both jamming in a parking lot between sets of a Bill Monroe show. They became fast friends, and influenced one another in many ways over the coming years. Grisman remembers, "He knew American music. He knew bluegrass, he knew rock and roll, he knew rhythm and blues, and he knew jazz. He turned me on to a million things."

Garcia, like many of Grisman's other collaborators, friends, and mentors, was older than he was. "I have always tried to be the youngest guy in the band, but it's getting more difficult," Grisman quips with a playful laugh. "It's been a great process, and now I find myself surrounded more often by younger people."

Grateful to still be playing the music he loves alongside players often 50 years his junior, Grisman continues, "I've got something for them, and I can also learn something from them. You've got to keep an open mind."

Tradition Starts as Heresy

Like J.S. Bach, whom he mentioned three times in an interview about his closest influences, Grisman started his career studying at the feet of master composers and performers. Like Bach, Grisman is a master of classical styles of his art form – in his case, bluegrass, jazz, and other forms of music. But, also like Bach, he has always pushed the boundaries, while never losing the heart and soul of the tune and harmony. What is Grisman's take on Bach and all his other disruptive forebears in music? "Tradition starts as heresy," he says.

Grisman was drawn quickly into the heretical haunts of bluegrass and old-time music. Admittedly a history buff, he recounts the story of how Bill Monroe broke boundaries with his rollicking music on the Grand Ole Opry stage. He then talks excitedly about the power that groups of autonomous, ingenious, and like-minded musicians are able to wield. "It was really revolutionary for Bill Monroe to hire Earl Scruggs on banjo in 1946. But he heard something in his playing that he could use."

Through the process of configuring and re-configuring his quartet and other ensembles, Grisman has similarly sought out such revolutionary souls. "Once they show up, you use them," he says. "I heard something in Tony Rice, Darol Anger, Todd Phillips, and Mike Marshall. In a way, my quintet started a revolution."

Despite the clear innovation that Monroe, Grisman, and other band leaders have brought to their music, their roots are still firmly planted in traditional soil. Grisman respectfully notes, "These were all elements that had been around for years." Regarding his own mandolin styles, he credits some of his predecessors. "Jethro Burns recorded jazz on the mandolin, Dave Apollon recorded everything on the mandolin," he notes, and Grisman is always careful to cite his sources, as he stands on the shoulders of giants.

However, he remembers that, for his late mentor Bill Monroe, the legendary mandolinist and "father of bluegrass," "bluegrass was 'it,' the greatest music on the face of the Earth, and he would never admit to being influenced by anything else." Grisman doesn't fault his teacher for this. "People will get interested in a style: rock and roll, grunge, swing, bebop, bluegrass, or old-time music. Then they kind of get entrenched. That's it. They don't really explore other styles." Grisman closes this thought by saying, "That's fine." But that "entrenched" place is certainly not where he or his bandmates and collaborators reside.

Dawg music lives on a tightrope between genres and represents a spectrum of melodic styles, from fast to slow, soft to loud, and ancient to modern. And Grisman's music gets better with

age, like a Lloyd Loar mandolin. "Music is an old art form, you know," he says. "And the greatest ingredient in music is time. Not just rhythm, and not just the keeping of time. I mean the cumulative effect of a lifetime of experience."

More Dissonance

Grisman came to an important conclusion in the 1960s: "I recognized that the mandolin was something that could probably play anything, if the player could figure out how to do it. It doesn't have to be Italian music. It doesn't have to be bluegrass. It could be a ballad by Billy Strayhorn, or it could be 'Happy Birthday,' J.S. Bach, or anything. It took me a while to realize this. Once I got into jazz, I went out and bought an alto sax. I figured you had to play a jazz instrument to play jazz. But I had no ability on the alto sax."

After laughing, admitting he never took a lesson on the saxophone, Grisman recounts what he learned from his attempt: "It informed me that I should go back and become a mandolin player!

"It kind of forced me to do the work on the mandolin," he explains, "to try to play the same melodies on the instrument that I had some ability with. For some reason, I was able to make the mandolin sound good."

And one of the great musical partnerships Grisman's mandolin ever forged was with the unsurpassably talented guitar of Clarence White. He speaks of a break he was given when he was still a teenager. "I had a great opportunity in 1964," he says. "The Kentucky Colonels asked me to play a weeklong gig at the Gaslight Café, because Roland White's wife had just given birth." The members of the band slept on the floor of Grisman's apartment, and they performed two or three sets every night. When they returned to the apartment late at night, David would "sit up with Clarence until the wee, wee hours, just jamming."

Many mandolinists and guitarists would love to have been a fly on the wall for the meeting of those young minds in that Greenwich Village walk-up, on those long nights. "You know, I was 19," Grisman recalls, "and he was about 21.

"He would fuck with time, you know," he continues. "He really opened me up to a lot of things that are articulated certain ways. He would displace a melody over the bar line, and he did some other really unusual things. But he did it with such precision that you would never get lost."

For the next nine years, Grisman had many more opportunities to play alongside White, before the brilliant guitarist's tragic death in 1973 at the hands of a drunk driver. "I was fortunate to really get to know Clarence musically. And personally. And I really felt, after he was gone, that there was this kind of vacuum for several years."

Then, in 1967, singer and guitarist Peter Rowan, who had just left his tenure with Bill Monroe's Bluegrass Boys after two years, joined his friend Grisman for a new joint project, Earth Opera. Rowan remembers, "It had bluegrass feeling in it, but we were playing it all in what was legato, arpeggio chords rather than strummed chords, so that every note would ring out in a chord, rather than just the rhythm part. David played mandocello and mandolin and I played guitar, and we wrote all of the songs."

Rowan recalls that they were mentored by Grisman's old friend Ralph Rinzler. "We used to see Ralph on a daily basis," Rowan says. "I had moved up to Cambridge after I was with Bill Monroe, and I wanted to be among whatever was going on with my contemporaries – kids in their mid-20s. And Ralph came and listened to us in the little bedroom where we were rehearsing. He said, 'More dissonance.' He said, 'I want to hear more dissonance.'

"We did what Ralph said," he adds. "We threw it all in there. In fact, we got to the point in dissonance where we couldn't even handle it, we fell apart. He was definitely a father figure for us. You know, he was a mentor."

Grisman's ears are still ringing from his years playing with Earth Opera. "We used to open shows for the Doors," he says. "I'll never forget it. One time in Toronto, we used the Doors' amplifiers, and the notes were like trees. I had this ringing in my ears all night long." Grisman laughs as he describes the feeling of the temporary deafness in his ears. "It makes you question your existence," he says. "But you know, evidently there are a lot of musicians who can handle that, but I'm not one that ever wanted to."

Taking the Bull by the Horns

"My friend, the great banjo innovator Bill Keith, who sadly just passed away, hired me for his first album in the spring of 1975," Grisman says. "I flew into Washington, DC, late at night, and we immediately went to a friend's house and crashed. At eight in the morning, he woke me up. He said, 'Come on out here! You've got to meet Tony Rice!' I had never heard of Tony Rice, and I guess he had flown in early that morning. We sat down on the living room floor of these people's house, I took up my mandolin, and he had his guitar. He hit his first few notes, and I said, 'Clarence is back.'"

Grisman's friend and bandmate Clarence White had been killed only two years earlier. "It's not that [Tony] was exactly like Clarence," he says, "but he had that same kind of phrasing and exactness.

He continues. "Tony was sitting on the floor in the living room, and he said, 'So, what have you been up to lately?'"

Grisman pulled out a tape he had recently recorded with his group, the Great American Music Band. He remembers, "There were a bunch of people there, but Tony was the only one listening to it. He heard one or two

tunes, and said, 'I would give my left nut to play that music.'"

At that time, Rice was playing with Ricky Skaggs and J.D. Crowe and the New South but was listening to jazz on the side. Grisman recalls, "I kind of bridged the connection for that. He insisted that I change my itinerary and go back to Lexington, Kentucky, with him, so that I could start teaching him these tunes. I did that, and stayed several days there.

"[Then,] Tony kept calling me up and asking, 'When's the gig?' I said, 'What gig?' I didn't even have a band. John Hartford was the first one to tell me that I was going to have my own band. I didn't really see it."

Grisman didn't go looking for the band this time; the band came to him.

"I had this mandolin student, Todd Phillips," he says. "He was the ace student in my Sausalito class. And one day he brought over this violinist, Darol Anger, who had tapes of all of our Great American Music Band stuff, and had learned all of Richard Greene's solos to my tunes." The David Grisman Quintet started to form, but they didn't have a guitarist – only two mandolins and a fiddle.

"Later that year, J.D. Crowe's band was going on a Japan tour," Grisman says, "and they had a gig in San Francisco the night before they were going to leave. I told Tony, 'Well, why don't you come out here a few days before that, and we'll rehearse?' Well, he came out, we got together, and then he played the gig in San Francisco. They went off to Japan the next day.

"A week later, the phone rings, and it was Tony Rice. I could tell he had a few sakes under his belt. And he told me he just gave J.D. his notice. He wanted to play my music; there was no stopping him. I never asked him to leave J.D. or anything like that." Grisman chuckles. "I thought, hey, at that point, I better take the bull by the horns. These guys have all volunteered."

After a brief pause for breath, he adds, in a playful voice, "You know, Tony

Rice named my band. I expected him to sing, you know. Here's this guy who is not only the world's greatest bluegrass guitar player, he also sings like a bird. I just figured it would be more of a collaboration. But he said, 'No, I came here to play your music. This is the David Grisman Quintet.'"

Good Music and the Other Kind

Since his experiment with Peter Rowan in Earth Opera came to a close in 1969, Grisman has rarely picked up an electric instrument. He founded Acoustic Disc Records in 1990, with the intention of putting out "100% handmade music." This has included some of the great players of several generations, and continues to be an important record label for acoustic music. The company's AcousticOasis.com features downloads of remastered versions of legendary recordings, including its latest release: the remastered version of the seminal 1991 album *Bluegrass Reunion*, featuring two previously unreleased tracks that include vocals by Jerry Garcia.

With respect to his record company, Grisman talks about the new reality of music sales. "With YouTube and streaming services, nobody really needs to buy music anymore," he says. "I mean, you can pay ten bucks a month and have access to however many millions of songs. And that's certainly enough for most people, and I understand that. But I have had to try to reinvent my career.

"I can't even call this the 'music business,'" he adds. "I'll call it the 'entertainment business.' Unfortunately, the commercial end of this thing has proliferated and had its effect on the music. It's not rooted in music, it's rooted in sales.

"One myth they have promoted, and in many cases have accomplished, is that music is disposable," he adds. "This week's music is like a hamburger. Next month, forget about it. It will be gone and replaced by something more current. And that's bullshit. J.S. Bach is just as valid today as he ever was. So is Uncle Dave Macon. Unfortunately, the business end of music has mandated that in order to keep selling music, they have to get rid of the old music, downplay it, or ignore it.

"The truth is, the world doesn't really need any more music," he continues. "There's so much great music that is available on recordings now, that you, I, and ten more people couldn't listen to it all in our collective lifetimes. So why do we need a bunch of guys with crazy hair and fucking rings coming out of their noses on some late night TV show playing a bunch of garbage? We don't need that. We should be listening to Duke Ellington. They should have Sonny Rollins on there, man. They should do a tribute to Bill Monroe. They should do a tribute to Earl Scruggs. They should do a fucking tribute to J.S. Bach. Instead you get some bunch of lame crap.

"Some of this music I'm talking about is, I believe, perfected. You know, perfect singing and all the rest. But it's soulless stuff, man. And we really don't need it. But the people who sell this stuff need to keep making millions of dollars on something, and they have to perpetuate the myth that this is something new, this is current, and this is what won the Grammy this year."

Grisman concludes, "They say a little bit of knowledge is a dangerous thing. Well, a lot of knowledge can also be dangerous. You know there's good and bad to all of this. It's a wonderful thing now that there's so much music available. You can just search the internet for Svend Asmussen, and if you've never heard of him, you can find out all about him. And if you get to hear his music, that's enough."

The Humanity of Acoustic Music

David Grisman started out like many of his peers did, hustling for gigs wherever he could find them. He worked with

Richard Greene, a fiddler, at the time, and neither of them was a singer. "You know, I didn't have this vision that I was going to make up a style of music called Dawg music, and that it was going to be instrumental, and that it was going to be my life's work," he says. "It kind of happened in an accidental way. … At some point, [Greene and I] decided that maybe we could make a go of it playing instrumentals."

Greene and Grisman explored their repertoire via a series of gigs and discovered that they would be able to craft great sets of music together. "We figured out right away that we just couldn't play fast fiddle tunes for 90 minutes, so we had to mix it up," Grisman says. "Of course, that's what jazz musicians had been doing for years. It was nothing new. But it had never been done that way with bluegrass instruments."

That was the beginning of what soon became Grisman's unique acoustic style of music. "Everybody's got a different take on what they want to accomplish. I basically wrote a lot of music," he says. "And guys like Tony Rice, Darol Anger, Mike Marshall, and others all dug that, and saw that as an outlet for their own expression."

Grisman has chosen to devote his career to the intricacies of acoustic music. "I love the sound of acoustic instruments. They are rooted in very old traditions. They've taken centuries to develop. And they were developed in a musical fashion."

He continues his melodic line of explanation: "If I go and buy Gibson's latest electric guitar, they won't even let me tune the damn thing; they've got these automatic tuning devices. The sound of that probably has a lot more to do with a computer chip from China than my touch. In fact, you can't hear it unless you plug it into an amp. Then, you're not hearing it come out of something you're holding. You're hearing it come out of a box that's somewhere else.

"It's so far removed from the humanity that is the most necessary ingredient in

the making of music. … Real music is not a bunch of guys cutting an instrumental track, and then two months later, carefully putting a vocal over it," he adds. "To me, [that's] not music. … It's kind of sad to me that most of what's called 'acoustic' isn't really acoustic, it's more like semi-acoustic – it's plugged-in. It's all about acoustic instruments with a pick-up on them, or some kind of attached microphone. And that, really, is all about volume. Unfortunately, we've gotten used to music that is really so loud, it's painful.

"I don't get why music should be painful. Maybe I have sensitive ears. But think about this, when it's that loud, it's crazy: why would a musician whose ears are finely tuned put stuff in their ears to protect them from the music?" Grisman laughs. "It just doesn't make any sense to me."

All Who Have a Large Vocabulary

In February 2002, in the lobby of a convention center, Grisman was standing with his mandolin strung around his neck, enraptured by the tunes that he was sharing with a small boy half his size. The boy was trading licks with his new mentor, to the delight of the informal crowd that had gathered around. In the tradition of his own teachers, Ralph Rinzler, Bill Monroe, Frank Wakefield, and so many others, Grisman has been a mentor and a father figure to generations of mandolinists and acoustic musicians.

He recalls meeting one of the world's greatest mandolinists, Chris Thile, when Thile was just eight years old, in 1989. Twenty-seven years later, Grisman still calls him a kid. "He's bringing the mandolin places it's never been before," Grisman says. "Chris Thile is a monster talent."

After noting that each generation has more technical ability than the previous, he says of Thile, "He's very curious, and he is also very thoughtful. He knows that he can play a million notes, but that's not what makes music."

"The greatest ingredient in music is time. Not just rhythm, and not just the keeping of time. I mean the cumulative effect of a lifetime of experience."

David Grisman

Making a play on words based on Thile's 2001 album *Not All Who Wander Are Lost* – which Thile took from a poem in *The Lord of the Rings* by J.R.R. Tolkien – Grisman speaks about musicians who have chops but no soul: "I would rephrase Chris' album title and say, 'All who have large vocabularies aren't necessarily poets.'

"Years ago, Chris asked me, 'How do you always sound like you?' Because he was kind of searching for his own sound," Grisman says. "I told him, 'It's inside you. You just have to come to that point. I didn't always sound like me either."

With that, Grisman summarizes his full and ongoing career. "I've kind of always looked at the big picture," he says. "And I've just made it through. I'm 70 years old and I'm probably working more than ever. I've hung in there and I've stayed true to what I do.

"I think music is a joyful experience, even if you're playing something sad," he adds. "It's an emotional experience. You can't take emotion out of music. It's part of it. No matter what else is involved, we're all doing something that we love to do."

So many mandolin players and instrumentalists have been influenced by Dawg and his music that it would be difficult to neatly trace his picking progeny. The branches of his musical family tree look more like alveoli, carrying oxygen through tiny capillaries into the blood cells of the giant, breathing organism of acoustic music.

After dozens of records over a half-century in music, David Grisman's Sextet is celebrating four decades of Dawg music, and they are releasing a new recording with some of their best, unreleased material: "It's the 40th year of my ensemble," he says. "Nine original

tunes will be on the record that have never been recorded by the band.

"My sextet now consists of George Cole on guitar and Chad Manning on fiddle, two relative newcomers compared with our bassist, Jim Kerwin, who has been playing with me for 30 years. Matt Eakle, our flute player, has been with us for 25 years. George Marsh, our percussionist, has played with me over two centuries now – he was in the band during the 1980s, and he's been with us for a decade during this century. This is a band that includes both Dawg veterans and relatively new guys.

"I think this is a realized sound – the culmination of what I've been doing for the past 40 years.

"Not that it's going to stop anytime in the near future," Dawg quickly adds. "I certainly hope not." ∎

PAST, PRESENT, FUTURE

**Darol Anger bows
to innovation**

by Lee Zimmerman

FIDDLE VIRTUOSO DAROL ANGER doesn't possess a time machine, but in many ways his music seems to travel through time, often within one song. His reverence for the roots of American music, particularly traditional music, manifests in every project he's ever been involved with. Yet, as an authentic Americana master, he's also been instrumental in pushing the parameters forward.

"I've always loved exploring the possibilities of different instruments," he says. "Certainly the violin has been an outsider instrument in music for a very long time, but during the last half of the 20th century, in particular, it made inroads into every kind of music. Even in country music, the fiddle was kind of on the outs for a while, but these days it's everywhere – not only in country, but in pop music as well. People try to break music into different genres, but I appreciate the people that can move the music forward."

Indeed, it's been the pursuit of music's possibilities – even as lessons from the past loom – that defines Anger's role as a musical mentor. It was also the thing that first inspired him to start playing. That and the Beatles.

Anger discovered the Fab Four when he was 11 years old. His interest in their music drew him to the guitar, until he was given a violin as a gift. He wasn't sure what to make of it at first. "That kind of music certainly wasn't something I was hearing on the radio," he remembers. "But I found that it was something I enjoyed, even though I was a classic violin failure by the time I was 14. I knew that playing strict classical music was not something I really wanted to do."

He eventually reverted back to guitar. "Applying the lessons I learned on the violin gave me a systematic approach to my playing," he explains. "I taught myself to play by ear, and I took my inspiration from the Beatles because they had that eclectic spirit. Pop music was exploding with so much possibility in the late '60s. There were no boundaries."

It also helped that he grew up in San Francisco. There, he happened upon the local band Seatrain, fronted by vocalist/guitarist Peter Rowan and fiddler Richard Greene, whose music gave him cause to revisit the violin. Then the song "Darkness Darkness" by the Youngbloods, with its sweeping strings, pushed him over the edge. "It was one of the great moments of my life," he says. "I decided 'I want to learn to play violin like that.'"

Further exploration brought him to bluegrass, the Rowan Brothers, and eventually, in 1977, the David Grisman Quintet, of which he was a founding member. That band helped establish the critical bridge between traditional bluegrass and the roots music that began appealing not only to Anger, but to a younger and more modern audience in general.

"There were a million guitar players all competing around the same time," he chuckles. "So I figured if I could learn to excel on violin, I'd have my own niche."

Once he carved that path for himself, other inroads followed. He played in a chamber jazz ensemble called Turtle Island String Quartet in 1985 and participated in various collaborations with fellow Grisman alumnus and mandolin virtuoso Mike Marshall. He fiddled his way through classical jazz efforts with pianist Barbara Higbie and their group Montreux for Windham Hill Records. There was his experimental bluegrass band Psychograss, the fusion ensemble Republic of Strings, and his seemingly never-ending collaborations, which have included time with notables like Stephane Grappelli, Bill Evans, members of Nickel Creek and Punch Brothers, Mark O'Connor, Bela Fleck, and Tony Rice. Outside of performing, he teaches at the Berklee College of Music, provides online lessons, and designs custom violins.

"Well, I guess I am busy," he laughs. "But I'm not doing it all at the same time. I also rely on the power of music to do all that stuff. It's not that complicated, really. I've played with a lot of people for a very long time. ... The relationships remain intact and the bonds are very strong." Still, it's hard not to get the impression that Anger is an extremely efficient multitasker. No sooner does he transition away from one project than he finds something new to dive into.

> "Applying the lessons I learned on the violin gave me a systematic approach to my playing. I taught myself to play by ear, and I took my inspiration from the Beatles because they had that eclectic spirit. ... There were no boundaries."
>
> Darol Anger

The Rise of Mr. Sun

Since 2013, he's been amassing a new ensemble, which now includes vocalist/mandolin player Joe Walsh, guitarist Grant Gordy, and bassist Ethan Jodziewicz in a quartet they've christened Mr. Sun. Boasting strains of bluegrass proficiency with a decidedly innovative sensibility, the band released its first album, *The People Need Light*, on Compass Records late last year.

"Darol's talents come full circle on *The People Need Light*," says Alison Brown, renowned banjoist and Compass Records president. "Mr. Sun gives Darol the perfect vehicle to continue his journey of musical exploration. ... [Their] album is a reminder of Darol's importance in the world of acoustic instrumental music. Few players have remained so vital for so long."

That's a fact that hasn't been lost on Anger's Mr. Sun bandmates. "Darol has been a musical hero of mine for years," says Jodziewicz. "You hear of people first getting into Darol's music through his work with David Grisman, but I actually came to him through the Turtle Island route. I was a total geek for that stuff, it's all I listened to for a while. We even played several of their arrangements in my public school orchestras, and it just moved me like nothing I had heard before.

"[It] drove me to wonder what it would be like to play with him," he adds. "As I've found out, Darol is a genius ensemble player, and a kind soul. He knows just what the music needs at every moment, and has this way of making you feel like he's hanging onto every note you play – just listening so hard, reacting, and conversing fully and completely. He's an incredibly supportive person, and has been an enormously important mentor to me, both musically and in life."

Gordy describes the experience of playing with Anger as a mix of awe, excitement, and some slight intimidation, "I was so taken with David Grisman's Dawg music and everything connected to it in my teenage years that Darol quickly became a towering figure in my mind," he admits. "I have learned that, while he does possess all the attributes that make his pedigree so impressive – as an instrumental virtuoso, stylistic innovator, master collaborator, compositional genius – at the root of it all is just a deep reverence, curiosity, and joy for music. This makes him just so fun and constantly inspiring to play with.

"And [then there's] ... his generosity," he adds. "It's really a defining characteristic."

Joe Walsh concurs. "When we first started playing together years ago," he says, "it was easy to put pressure on myself to live up to the standard he sets, but he's so generous and supportive that he naturally makes everyone around him sound better."

Across Generations

Indeed, while Anger has pulled from a variety of musical threads – mostly jazz, folk, and classical – it's the merging of different generations that comes to the fore on Mr. Sun's debut. And Anger's enthusiasm encourages his younger bandmates to feel free to explore as well.

"I think what makes the band interesting – both for us musicians and for the audience – is that we have four very different, individual personalities at work," Gordy explains. "It works best when those elements are in balance, whether it's over the course of a set or within a single piece. Joe can always be counted on to have this rock-solid, hyper-aware snap of time feel in his mandolin playing, and Ethan brings his incredible precision, boundless technique, and steady feel to the bass. Darol can sing or sigh or scream on the fiddle, his expressive range moving from almost manic humor to intensely profound gravity."

That may be Anger's greatest gift. While his ability to tamper with the template, regardless of style and genre, is impressive, it's his unique style and influence on musicians of another generation – those that are following in his wake – that is especially noteworthy, particularly when it comes to taking the music into different realms.

"I suppose I have a restless spirit," Anger admits. "A lot of projects do overlap, but at this point I'm the senior member of my class, so I guess have the responsibility to help move it forward. There's this whole new wave of interesting players. Many of them not only have an interest in the music, but they've also done their homework."

He pauses, then adds, "Maybe it's just simple economics. I have been working with a lot of younger musicians over the past couple of decades, and younger musicians tend to move on. They pass through a stage and then do something else. So maybe that's part of it on some level. It feeds on itself. It's a circular thing. I can't pay people a retainer. ... That's why I enjoy teaching. It actually adds some stability to my life." ∎

ALTERNATE ROUTE

Tim O'Brien finds new model and new muse *by Stacy Chandler*

YOU DON'T NEED A FANCY GET-UP to do what Tim O'Brien does. Over a career that's touched ground in five decades, he's shared songs penned by his own hand as well those of roots music's pioneers. He plays a multitude of instruments and often shares the stage with fellow artists whose love for the song and the playing flows straight through to the audience.

Granted, O'Brien appreciates a good costume – just ask his alter ego, Red Knuckles, who joins the Trailblazers to add literal and figurative color to Hot Rize shows. But he most often performs in a casual shirt and jeans or, when playing with the Earls of Leicester, a black suit with string tie. Still, he was inspired by a bad hair day to write the title track of his most recent album, last year's *Pompadour*.

For most of us, waking up with funky hair means you heave a sigh and reach for a hat, or maybe some product. But that's not how O'Brien copes. Instead, he turns a bad-hair day into a catchy song that ponders life's could-have-beens. In the album's title track, he croons:

I started thinking different
about how I'd spend my day
I would need a suit of rhinestones,
that would be the only way.

O'Brien affirms he wrote the song based on a true-life bedhead experience. "People spend hundreds, thousands of dollars on salon care to get that the way it was," he says with a laugh, describing what he saw in the mirror. Luckily, he didn't go so far as to give his life over to rhinestones. But could-have-beens are always turning over in O'Brien's musical mind, it seems, and he's got a special knack for turning them into gotta-be's.

Conquering Contrasts

In a way, *Pompadour*, released last October on O'Brien's own Howdy Skies Records, was as much of a surprise as that short-lived hairdo that gave the album its title.

Even though his previous solo album, *Chicken & Egg*, was more than four years in the rearview, O'Brien didn't see a lot of space in his calendar to make a new one. He was busy with collaborations with longtime friend Darrell Scott; recording and performing with Earls of Leicester, the Jerry Douglas-led supergroup that pays tribute to Flatt & Scruggs; and the new era of Hot Rize with Pete Wernick, Nick Forster, and Bryan Sutton. But he did have a chance to grab some music-making time with New Zealand guitarist Gerry Paul and bassist Trevor Hutchinson from Ireland.

"I love getting in the studio and just sort of getting my feet wet and seeing what will happen," O'Brien says. "This is the product of just a couple of friends getting together to have some fun. We thought we might turn it into something as a common project between the three of us, but it just wasn't in the cards."

A new baby (in Paul's case), the distance between continents, and already packed touring schedules made a tour impossible, but that didn't mean the project was dead. O'Brien, not content

to let songs just sit, finished them up, and *Pompadour* was born.

The album catches a man in a moment when perspectives are shifting. You get the idea that O'Brien, 62, doesn't view life quite the same way as he did when he was, say, 22. In "Whatever Happened to Me," for example, a man reminisces on his earlier life – before a music career – then decides to consult a psychic. She leans over a crystal ball and asks, "Are you lookin' for someone?" And the chorus gives his reply:

My face in the mirror looks the
same each day
It's hard to see the changes when
you measure time that way
Whatever happened to me?

"I think you're always trying to be conscious of where you are in the scheme of things – in society and in the stages of life," says O'Brien. "You know, it's funny, you do the same things over and over as you go through your life, but as you get older, your perspective on them has changed. I'm not sure we ever really know where we are in this. I think we're always viewing it from a different angle as we go through it."

In addition to aging, one big perspective-changer in O'Brien's life was the end of his marriage a few years back, and then the start of a new relationship with Jan Fabricius, who manages his office and appears on *Pompadour* with background vocals as well as in the lyrics to "I'm a Mess for You."

But it's not all deep thoughts and introspection. There are plenty of moments of fun on *Pompadour*, that spark of wit that fans have always appreciated about O'Brien.

It's hard not to raise an eyebrow, though, when you see "Get Up Offa That Thing" on the track list. Yes, it's *that* "Get Up Offa That Thing," by James Brown – a bold choice, perhaps, for a red-headed, acoustic-leaning folksinger. But it works. With bass, banjo, guitar, and a touch of Hammond organ, the groove gets simplified. O'Brien keeps it laid back with casual "good gawd y'alls" and adds some down-home verses. It's a good time, but it's far from a novelty song. If Brown set out to make you feel better, O'Brien is carrying the torch, even as he brings a very different vibe to the song.

"Some bluegrass is the funkiest music there is," he explains. "The mandolin is one of the funkiest instruments there is – it can really play unusual rhythms if you let it. I've never had a sense of the borders between music as much as others, I suppose. I don't really think about music as being in various categories – I just play it. When you stumble on those things that are so obviously incongruent, sometimes you have to look at them and say, 'Well, wait, *are* they incongruent?'"

O'Brien didn't let the idea of incongruence stop him from making *Red on Blonde*, a 1996 album of Bob Dylan songs set against a bluegrass background, or *Reincarnation*, a 2012 tribute album of Roger Miller's songs, performed with his sister Mollie and other musical family members.

"When you see something that seems like such a high contrast, you might consider how those contrasting things would fit together," he says. But he's not given to over-analyzing it. "Mostly it's just borne out of some fun." And with the James Brown cover in particular: "It's just about the joy of playing a groove."

To Know Where We're Going

While his covers of James Brown and Bob Dylan are of relatively recent vintage, O'Brien can and often does reach much farther back for songs to mix into his repertoire.

"The old songs, they have a context that's built around them, the older they are," he says. "When you sing a song like 'The Weight' by The Band, you're putting yourself in a whole bag of things, and you're calling attention to the whole mood that has coalesced around that song over the decades. And with an old ballad, sometimes … you go, 'Gee, it kind of tells the story that we're still going through today.'"

Besides addressing age-old stories around love, war, and death, those old songs also strike a chord in us that goes deeper than words.

"It helps us know where we're going if we can tell where we came from. There's a nostalgia to it, and sort of an escapism to it. It's not unlike my attraction to Irish music: it's kind of exotic, and yet it's very familiar. The old songs are kind

> # "The mandolin is one of the funkiest instruments there is – it can really play unusual rhythms if you let it."
>
> Tim O'Brien

of familiar even if you didn't really think you knew them. You kind of hear these melodies, [and] it's something in your collective consciousness or your DNA."

As technology changes and the way we consume music along with it, O'Brien has found there's one thing that stays the same: the power of making music – and listening to music being made – as a means of finding common ground.

"Just the very act of making music is kind of a communal thing, like making a fire and telling a story," he says. "It's kind of a thing we do as humans that defines us. It's like the myths of each culture – they tell the story, they make sense of things for people, they kind of draw the chaos of life together in some sort of meaning. The new songwriters are trying to do the same thing. They're not doing anything different. They've just got slightly new materials to work with."

And there is plenty of new ground to cover, which is why there's always room for new songs, new genres, and new approaches to making music.

"You can't get away from the past," he says, "but you also can't help but be in the present and point toward the future."

The End of the Album?

Over his long career, O'Brien has seen a lot of changes in the music business. Trends have come and gone (as have hairstyles), and audiences have changed the way they listen to – and support – musicians like him.

"I kind of wondered if I'd ever make a record again," he says. It's not that he was ready to hang up his guitar (or fiddle, or banjo, or mandolin), but rather that he didn't see records – in the traditional sense

of collections of songs around a certain theme, story, mood, or vibe – as what listeners wanted from him, necessarily.

He knew that, especially to many of today's listeners who rely on streaming services, the song's the thing. So he started Short Order Sessions, which offers new songs on a regular basis – one or two a month – for purchase as singles through digital platforms such as iTunes and Amazon.

"I knew I was going to keep recording, and that's why I started Short Order Sessions, to see if there's another way to keep active without trying to promote a disc," he explains. He was also inspired by Folkways Records – which prioritized the importance of cataloging songs without regard to theme, timing, or commercial viability – as well as by his own love for streaming music.

"If I'm reading my biography of Louis Armstrong and I want to hear the songs that they discuss, maybe I can find them on Spotify," he says, making clear he's drawn by the service's convenience, but not so much by its model for paying musicians. He tends to use it, he admits, even when he wants to listen to something already in his physical collection. "I thought, 'Gee, this really is a more convenient model.'"

Sometimes the SOS songs feature him alone, and sometimes they capture musical sessions that ensue at his house when friends' tours bring them through Nashville. The lovingly humorous "Dance You Hippy Dance" was an early offering, and he's also put out a Christmas song and a lovely version of "Brother Can You Spare a Dime?"

"I like the idea that there's not a lot of import put on this," he says. "It's just like, 'This is what I do with my days.'

And you don't say, 'Well, this is my grand statement that I'm going to make this year.'" He likens the abbreviated process to the time-honored practice of working songs out on stage: "I'm trying things out and I adjust as I go."

In addition to freeing him from having to come up with a certain number of songs that fit some certain theme, SOS also lends some immediacy to his tunes. He can react to current events – he wrote about West Virginia's Elk River chemical spill in 2014, and the habitual escapee from police custody who stole Crystal Gayle's tour bus in a quest to visit his dying mama in 2007. Or he can simply capture a mood as it bubbles up and get those songs out into the world with little delay.

The freedom SOS gives is powerful, O'Brien says. "I can't decide whether I want to make a hundred records or no records, because I can't decide what the next one is going to be. ... [With SOS] anything goes, and it doesn't have to be related to anything that went before it in any particular way."

O'Brien sees it as a workable blueprint for artists making their way in an uncertain future. But, he concedes, you never can tell.

"Every time you make a new record, it's a different story. And every time you go into the marketplace, it seems to be a little different story. The one thing remains the same, which is that musicians, artists, they want to comment on their lives, they want to communicate. I guess we're there to provide a focal point for people who are not thinking that way. They're mostly going through their lives, and we give them a chance to slow down and take a look at what's been happening." ∎

BIGGER
AND
BOULDER

Colorado's Railsplitters
travel their own road
by David McPherson

L to R: Christine King, Dusty Rider, Lauren Stovall, Peter Sharpe, Leslie Ziegler.

IN HIS INTRODUCTION TO *THE Bluegrass Reader*, Thomas Goldsmith writes: "In an age when musical trends flit by like models on a Paris runway, bluegrass has endured – and changed – certainly long enough for its history to have a shape."

Now into that history – and out of this world – go the Railsplitters, carving their own musical shapes and sounds. Always bending and blending disparate elements, the Boulder, Colorado-based five-piece takes nods from progressive bluegrass innovators such as Punch Brothers, Joy Kills Sorrow, Yonder Mountain String Band, Lake Street Dive, and Crooked Still. Dig deeper into the twisting roots of this band's musical family tree and you find traces of David Grisman, Tony Rice, and even Bill Monroe. Like many of their generation, the Railsplitters are adding to the musical forms of the past, finding ways to innovate those sounds.

"Tilt-A-Whirl," the lead cut on their *The Faster It Goes* album, which they self-released in 2015, is a fitting metaphor. With both the music and the ride, you never know in what direction you might get spun next. No two listens will be the same, thanks in no small part to the creative genius of banjoist Dusty Rider and his arrangements that experiment with unconventional time signatures and tempos.

"We all come from varying backgrounds," says Rider, who cites both Gorillaz and the Infamous Stringdusters as influences. "I grew up playing banjo much the same way Earl Scruggs did, until I figured out that there were other ways to play it ... more technically interesting ways. Our music, especially in the context of US bluegrass music, means different [things] depending on where you are."

Joining Rider in the Railsplitters are fiddler Christine King, mandolinist Peter Sharpe, bassist Leslie Ziegler, and guitarist and singer Lauren Stovall, whose angelic, captivating voice is as much a part of the band's distinct sound as is its instrumentation. But, while innovative bluegrass is somewhat of the norm on the modern stringband scene, the way this particular group has come together and evolved has been the fuel that feeds their stirring sounds.

Born in Boulder

At the base of the foothills of the Rocky Mountains, 25 miles northwest of Denver, sits the music-loving town of Boulder, Colorado. Its bluegrass scene is rich and collaborative, with picking parties happening somewhere most nights. Each member of the Railsplitters moved to Boulder to get in on the action. Stovall, originally from Jackson, Mississippi, moved there about five years ago from Aspen, where she first dug into bluegrass.

"Yonder Mountain String Band was my gateway drug into bluegrass," she says. "In Aspen, my discovery came at the Great Divide music shop. That's also when I first heard about what a bluegrass jam was, and started to tag along with friends. ... Then, I came to Boulder to find work, thought it was a cool town, and started to go to jams and play."

Sharpe, who grew up on the Connecticut coast, has lived in Boulder the longest of anyone in the band. He moved there in 1999, following his love of climbing and skiing. His path to bluegrass was accidental. While he had played other stringed instruments

"I grew up playing banjo much the same way Earl Scruggs did, until I figured out that there were other ways to play it."

Dusty Rider

since grade school, he first picked up the mandolin in college when he found his great-grandfather's pre-war Gibson under his parents' bed. "I mostly got into bluegrass via the mandolin," he says. "I had these mandolins fall into my lap. ... I was a big Deadhead in high school. [Then,] in college, I heard Grisman and Garcia, through that route. That was my gateway drug. ... It was only years later that I discovered Monroe and all the other traditional stuff."

Ziegler, meanwhile, hails from Michigan via West Virginia. While attending college at Western Michigan University in Kalamazoo, she immersed herself in the local scene and discovered a fondness for bluegrass and folk music. This love eventually brought her to the Rocky Mountains, where she found she could further explore that scene.

Rider's musical education began in Upstate New York. A stint in Anchorage, Alaska, working the railroad as a brakeman gave him time in the evenings to hone his five-string skills, playing in the band High Lonesome Sound. A stop in Oklahoma City followed, before he settled into Boulder in 2011. From the moment Rider arrived, he witnessed the town's incredible, inclusive acoustic music community. "It's very collaborative and everyone shares ideas and music," he says. "I had never walked into a music community that was as inviting, helpful, and supportive."

Finally, King is the only Colorado native in the band – she was born and raised in Denver. She picked up the violin in second grade and it wasn't long before she discovered Texas-style fiddling.

Though Rider and Ziegler first met at RockyGrass, it was at Boulder's nightly jams where members of the Railsplitters first shared a stage. But the band's story officially began on a night in January 2012,

when Stovall had a solo gig and decided she wanted to add in some friends she had met in the local jam scene. She dubbed the band Lauren & Friends, and went for it.

"We just sort of ran with it initially," she says. "There was no long-term plan. We said, let's try it for three months, see how it feels, and then decide whether we [should] keep going. Well, three months went by and we never even had the conversation about quitting."

Bassist Ziegler, who cites Edgar Meyer as an inspiration, came up with the name. "The mascot of one of my neighboring high schools was the Lincoln Railsplitters," she says. "When we were throwing out names, I put it on the table." Then, like a true 21st-century musician, she adds, "The real moment was when we found out therailsplitters.com was not taken."

Going Faster

The Railsplitters released their self-titled debut a year later and then followed it last year with *The Faster It Goes*. The latter features 11 songs that take listeners on a journey down some dusty roads that hint at a time long past, even as they coast down a modern highway. The band's musicianship is on full display in the instrumental "Goosetown," penned by Sharpe. They reinvent traditional tunes like "Salt Salt Sea" and chug along like a train running the rails on originals like "Planted on the Ground." It's all part of the journey, and this forlorn, oft-lonely road traverses the graves of bluegrass brethren gone.

But to truly *get* the Railsplitters' ethos, one must see them live.

"A lot of times in acoustic music, it can feel like musicians are onstage and the audience is off the stage watching," Stovall explains. "We try to honor the

space that is created between the two, because we are really trying to share something more than the music and make it a participatory experience."

"We really try to model our shows after the Infamous Stringdusters and the energy they have on stage," King adds. "If anyone ever asks me what people are going to walk away with from our live show, I tell them it's the vocal harmonies. All five of us sing, so four- or five-part harmony is a strong and unique feature of some of our songs."

Stovall admits that, every once in a while, Rider will write a song that pushes the bluegrass boundaries a bit too far. "We will be like, 'That's a little too weird,'" she says. "We have to rein it in, tone it down a bit, so people can relate to it and groove to it."

The reins they hold seem to be doing the trick. Looking back, 2015 was the band's busiest year yet. Fans started to groove to their inventive sounds and everyone in the band dropped their day jobs. "We are all full-time musicians now," says Stovall. "It was a great year to promote *The Faster It Goes*, but there was a large gap between our first two records, and we don't want that large gap to go by this time around."

So, as summer approaches, the Railsplitters are planning time in the studio to record an EP, along with possibly a live record curated from one of their gigs last year in Germany.

Like the early American pioneers who split the rails to forge a communication link between East and West, North and South, from sea to sea, the Railsplitters are building their own links with listeners, continuing to push traditional bluegrass boundaries while staying true to the genre's roots – one song, one note, one memorable riff, and one heartfelt harmony at a time. ∎

L to R: Jeremy Darrow, Adam
Roszkiewicz. Melody Walker,
Leif Karlstrom, Jacob Groopman

ROLL WITH THE PEOPLE I KNOW

Front Country takes off
by Deborah Crooks

ON AN UPWARD AND INCREASINGLY visible trajectory since the band began to coalesce in 2011, Front Country has been heralded as one of the top new bluegrass bands by folks like the BBC's Bob Harris and Railroad Earth's Tim Carbone. They won the 2013 Telluride Band Competition, after taking home the same honor the year before at RockyGrass, and have shared stages with bluegrass greats like Laurie Lewis and Peter Rowan, all while sticking to their more wide-ranging musical sensibilities.

Their Kai Welch-produced debut, *Sake of the Sound* (2014), presented a collection of original songs and instrumental compositions, as well as covers of bluegrass stalwarts, contemporary songwriters, and traditional gospel tunes. The disc is a snapshot of Front Country's considerable capabilities, and its title track just might be their manifesto. More of a rock anthem than what one might expect from a stringband, the lyrics spell out exactly who Front Country is: a highly-adept band forged amid geologic fault lines and multicultural edges, whose members live for playing music.

Feel the room shake
Hear my heart break
I'm in love with the sound
The love that we make
We make for our sake
For the sake of the sound

The love and determination in that song is characteristic of Front Country, as are guts, hard work, tenacity, and talent. Led by singer Melody Walker and multi-instrumentalist Jacob Groopman, they are rounded out by mandolinist Adam "Roscoe" Roszkiewicz, fiddler Leif Karlstrom, and bassist Jeremy Darrow. A typical performance finds them laying claim to rock and roll and jazz as much as traditional folk and bluegrass. That array of sounds is no surprise, considering Walker and Groopman's backgrounds.

Becoming a Band

Walker grew up a musician's daughter, surrounded by songs and songwriting in Martinez, California. "My parents took me to Strawberry [Music Festival] each year," she says over the phone, recalling her influences. "I grew up listening to Laurie Lewis and Kathy Kallick and Peter Rowan."

After learning guitar and piano from her father, Walker went on to major in music at Humboldt State University in Arcata, California, where she co-founded a women's global fusion a cappella group called AkaBella.

She and Groopman met at a gig in 2010, when Groopman was playing with an Afrobeat band and Walker's band was playing Balkan music. Incongruous as that first meeting may have been, it quite accurately represents the searching curiosity that underpins Front Country's sound. Despite the styles in which they were embedded at the time, the pair quickly realized they both loved bluegrass and shared even more common ground elsewhere.

Growing up in Virginia, Jacob Groopman discovered guitar at age 12. He veered toward the Grateful Dead and bluegrass during high school, then majored in jazz at the Oberlin Conservatory of Music. Nonetheless, he remained drawn to bluegrass. "The vibe of the bluegrass scene, it's all about music," he says. "There's not a lot of ego. It's a lot more laid back than jazz, but the musicianship is incredible."

While at Oberlin, Groopman found himself in classes with guitarist Chris Eldridge, who started his career with progressive bluegrass band the Infamous Stringdusters before joining the genre-transcendent Punch Brothers. It was Eldridge who nurtured Groopman's love of bluegrass by showing him the basics of bluegrass guitar.

After graduation, Groopman moved to San Francisco with a jug band called Jug Free America, who chose the Bay Area for its diversity. Between the time when that group – which lasted "about a year" – split up and Front Country developed, Groopman did a four-year stint as guitarist for the touring Afrobeat ensemble Albino!

Still, bluegrass remained his touchstone. When not on the road with Albino!, Groopman worked at 5th String Music Store in Berkeley and taught music. "The 5th String was kind of the center of the bluegrass scene in the East Bay," he says. "So even when I was playing in a lot of other bands, I kept my foot in the door."

Between gigs, he went to local jams and became an in-demand player and respected music teacher. Spurred by meeting Walker, he quit Albino! in 2010 to concentrate on bluegrass full-time, and the duo quickly began to collaborate with serious intent.

He added mandolin, guitar, and vocals to Walker's early solo efforts – 2011's *III* EP and 2012's *Gold Rush Goddess*. In 2013, San Francisco-based bluegrass legend Laurie Lewis produced their acoustic duo release *We Made It Home*, another polished and eclectic collection of originals and covers. That disc highlights Groopman's multi-instrumentalism, Walker's intelligent writing, and the duo's easy chemistry. They followed with a tour and, somewhere between the road and the studio, Front Country was born in a San Francisco cafe.

"Our original banjo player, Jordan Klein, had a monthly, three-hour bluegrass gig at the Atlas Cafe [in San Francisco's Mission District]," Groopman remembers. "He invited me along with Roszkiewicz to help fill out the time. I invited Melody because she had great songs and a better voice than any of us."

Indeed, Walker is that golden combination of someone who can write and play as well as she can interpret songs. Covering The Dead's "Loser" and singing "Good Lovin'" and "Second that Emotion" during a recent Grateful Dead tribute at San Francisco's Great American Music Hall, she called to mind a powerful combination of Susan Tedeschi and Sharon Jones, confidently fronting the band while mining the depths of each lyric. A dedicated songwriter, she also earned top honors in the Chris Austin

"Getting to play Telluride, with thousands of people in the audience, validated what we were doing."

Melody Walker

Songwriting Contest at MerleFest in 2013, and now contributes the majority of Front Country's originals. But back in 2011 at the Atlas Cafe, she was just making music with her friends. "We didn't have a name," she remembers. "I think it was called Free Live Bluegrass."

In addition to Walker's voice and Groopman's instruments, Roszkiewicz, a graduate of the San Francisco Conservatory of Music, brought with him his own musical pedigree and penchant for adventurous arrangements. This mix made Free Live Bluegrass one of the best tickets in town that year.

Powered by Bluegrass

The assemblage may not have had a solid name, but they had so much something, if ineffable and organic, that they took their show to RockyGrass and came away winners. "We were having a good time playing together," says Groopman. "Then we won RockyGrass and realized, 'Oh, this is something.'

"Nobody in the band grew up in bluegrass," he adds, name checking a diverse mix of classic and contemporary acts including Bonnie Raitt, Punch Brothers, Dawes, the Barr Brothers among their influences. He also names the Grateful Dead and Old and In the Way – the 1975 supergroup that brought together Jerry Garcia, David Grisman, Peter Rowan, Vassar Clements, John Kahn, Richard Greene, and John Hartford for one record (and a reunion album three decades later).

"All of us came from very diverse backgrounds," he concludes. "Melody was singing world music, I studied jazz, two of our bandmates studied classical."

Still, as broad-minded as their tastes are, Front Country is very much at home among bluegrass tradition and royalty. Walker now routinely shares stages with some of the same artists she watched play as a child. "Peter Rowan's a huge influence," she says. "We've opened for Peter a couple of times as a duo and have collaborated at the odd festival, since we frequently end up at similar events. It's amazing to hang out with a player like that, who's played with Bill Monroe and taken bluegrass all sorts of places."

Joining Lewis and Kallick among the others at a holiday show last December, Front Country had an air of being among relatives. Groopman donned a Santa suit midshow, and sang, along with Roszkiewicz and Kallick, Ralph Stanley's "Beautiful Star of Bethlehem." Walker also featured prominently, and remarkably, in most of the main sets – singing "Children Go Where I Send Thee" with Groopman and Lewis and a stunning version of Fleet Foxes' "White Winter Hymnal" with the T Sisters, before infusing Kallick's "Kissing Comes Easy" with a vocal that was as much torch as twang.

Front Country closed their set that night with another composition by Walker: "Family Band," a song that first appeared, prophetically, on her 2011 EP, well before the RockyGrass and Telluride wins and everything that has followed.

I wanna roll with the people I know
Truckin' through the rain and the
*   sleet and snow*
Smilin' through the pain 'cause it
*   makes us grow*
I wanna roll with the people I know

"I wrote 'Family Band' in 2010," she says. "It was one of those 'gift songs' that came out all at once. For a year I thought it was too simple and sentimental to get away with playing live, but we started doing it and the response was overwhelming."

It took a few years, but by 2015, Front Country nearly fully realized the song's directive. "There were a lot of changes [last year]," says Groopman, referring to a year that found them on the road nearly nonstop. "We made the decision to be a five-piece. Roscoe stepped in on harmonies and we hired [Jeremy Darrow], who is now our full-time bass player. It was a lot of pressure to get it together."

"Getting to play Telluride, with thousands of people in the audience, validated what we were doing," Walker adds, recognizing another pivotal moment in the band's ascent, which finds them looking at a rapidly filling 2016 schedule.

Indeed, the year kicked off for this band with a pair of Nevada shows supporting Leftover Salmon. There was an appearance at the Anchorage Folk Festival before they set out for an East Coast tour, trucking and rolling and picking and smiling with no end in sight. By February, Front Country was in the Rocky Mountains; and the summer calls for headlining La Roche Bluegrass Festival in France. Sometime this year, they're hoping to start working on the follow-up to *Sake of the Sound*, if they can find the time.

"[Front Country] is like a ship," says Groopman with a slight chuckle. "I'm keeping a handle on it, [but] it has a lot more power than I do. I just try to let it do its thing." ∎

Contributors

CARA GIBNEY writes about music and musicians for *No Depression*, *fRoots Magazine*, Americana UK, *CultureHub* Magazine, *Gigging NI*, and elsewhere. She lives in Belfast, Northern Ireland.

CAT JOHNSON is a freelance writer based in Santa Cruz, California. She writes about community, the commons, co-working, and music.

CHRIS WADSWORTH is a lifelong musician, founder of the FreshGrass Foundation, and publisher of *No Depression*. He lives in San Francisco with his kids and spends as much time as he can in Montana.

COLIN SUTHERLAND is an illustrator and designer living in the mountains of North Carolina. He finds inspiration in century-old fiddle tunes and vintage print ephemera.

DAVID McPHERSON is a freelance writer with more than 18,000 songs on his iPod and an ever-growing vintage vinyl collection. He lives in Canada with his wife and two children.

DEBORAH CROOKS is a California-based freelance writer and performing songwriter. Her work has appeared in *Northern Lights*, *Yoga Journal*, and the anthology *Bare Your Soul: The Thinking Girl's Guide to Enlightenment*.

DENIS GAINTY is a mandolin player and associate professor of history at Georgia State University in Atlanta. He's writing a book on the history of bluegrass music in Japan.

DREW CHRISTIE is a Seattle-based animator and illustrator. His work has been featured by *The New York Times*, *Huffington Post*, *The Atlantic*, and others.

ERIN LYNDAL MARTIN received her MFA in poetry from the University of Alabama. Her work has appeared in *The Rumpus*, *Salon*, *The Quietus*, and elsewhere.

GRANT BRITT writes about music and more from his home in Greensboro, North Carolina. You can find his rants and rambles in *Blues Music Magazine*, *O. Henry* magazine, *The Independent*, and *The Greensboro News and Record*.

GWENDOLYN ELLIOTT is a freelance writer and former music editor of *Seattle Weekly*. She lives in the Emerald City with her husband, pets, and a lot of vinyl records.

JASON GOODMAN is a photographer and visual artist who lives and works in Rockland, Maine.

JON LANGFORD is a founding member of the Mekons, Three Johns, and Waco Brothers, and an acclaimed visual artist. Born in South Wales, he currently lives and works in Chicago. He was a 2015 artist-in-residence at the Country Music Hall of Fame and Museum. The Waco Brothers' latest album, *Going Down in History*, was released in February on Bloodshot Records.

JOSHUA M. MILLER is a Wisconsin-based freelance writer. He covers the music scenes in Milwaukee and Madison and enjoys writing about a variety of genres.

JULIE WENGER WATSON is a Texan by birth and an Okie for life. She is co-director of the nonprofit Tulsa Roots Music and writes regularly for *Currentland*, *Northwest Arkansas Entertainment Magazine*, Red Dirt Nation, *TulsaKids* and *Intermission* magazine.

KELLY McCARTNEY is managing editor for the Bluegrass Situation. She regularly contributes to *No Depression*, Folk Alley, and *Curve*. She lives in Nashville, Tennessee.

LEE ZIMMERMAN has been a freelance writer for publications like *American Songwriter*, *Blurt*, and *Billboard* for 20 years. He lives in Maryville, Tennessee, with his wife.

KENT GUSTAVSON, Ph.D., is the author of the award-winning biography of Doc Watson, *Blind But Now I See* (Sumach-Red Books, 2012). He is a serial entrepreneur, and he currently lives in Bonn, Germany, with his wife, dog, two cats, and guitar.

KIM RUEHL is the editor of *No Depression*. Her work has appeared in *CityArts*, *Seattle Weekly*, *Billboard*, NPR, and elsewhere. She lives in Asheville, North Carolina, with her wife and kid.

MARC HARKNESS is a Panamanian-born graphic designer, illustrator, musician, and kayaker. He has designed album art for James McMurtry, Billy Joe Shaver, Jason Isbell, and Sarah Lee Guthrie and Johnny Irion, among others.

MIKE SEELY is a former editor of *Seattle Weekly*. He wrote about Lucinda Williams in *No Depression*'s 2015 issue and contributes regularly to the publication's website.

PHIL CLARKIN is a concert, people, and architecture photographer based in Tulsa, Oklahoma.

SCOTT ALARIK is a journalist, author, and singer-songwriter who covered folk music in the *Boston Globe* for over 20 years. He has authored two books – *Deep Community* and *Revival: A Folk Music Novel*, which won the Benjamin Franklin Silver Award for Popular Fiction.

STACY CHANDLER is the copy editor and social media manager for *No Depression*. She lives in Raleigh, North Carolina, with her husband, their daughter, a big dumb yellow dog, and an underused fiddle.

TIM DUFFY has been seeking out musicians who perform traditional music ever since he attended college in Swannanoa, North Carolina. He founded the Music Maker Relief Foundation in 1994 with his wife, Denise.

Screen Door

A NEW WAY FORWARD

BY CHRIS WADSWORTH

When FreshGrass acquired No Depression in 2014, the ND Community repeatedly asked us, "Who is FreshGrass and what is your mission?"

I can admit it now: initially these questions made us feel a little defensive because there were often undertones – and sometimes blatant accusations – of sinister or "corporate" poisoning of a beloved grassroots community and brand. But more importantly, it was awfully hard for us to ask people to get behind us when we weren't yet able to make a clear statement about who we were and where we were taking both FreshGrass and *No Depression*.

We made a lot of progress last fall, when we solidified our answer to the question of "What is *No Depression*?" (it's a music publication) with our first print edition since 2008. But the bigger questions – What is FreshGrass? How do FreshGrass and ND fit together? – were still dangling. Meanwhile, this whole time, we've been hard at work behind the scenes figuring out the answers to these questions. And the answer, it became clear, was the FreshGrass Foundation – a nonprofit whose mission is to preserve, promote, and create innovative grassroots music.

We want to cultivate deep roots, expand creative ideas, and help make FreshGrass the definitive roots music platform.

We're doing this with a combination of commercial endeavors and giving programs. Our flagship commercial offerings are: the FreshGrass Festival at MASS MoCA in North Adams, Massachusetts, each September; *No Depression* – our print and online publication (no intro needed if you're reading this); and our growing online store.

The FreshGrass Festival has come a long way in four years, and as it continues to gain a foothold in the New England festival season, we hope and plan to have at least one, if not more, FreshGrass festivals in other parts of the country.

No Depression has progressed in recent years as well, and its evolution has been well documented in these pages and online. Now we've taken one more giant leap, by committing to making this a quarterly print journal. The ND website will continue to support the journal by offering timely coverage of new releases, reviews, columns, video programs, and more, and to support the growing community of ND fans with a daily place to visit and interact with each other.

Finally, our online store will expand as we grow our library of new editions, branded items, original illustrations and art, and more.

Any and all profits from these commercial efforts will stay in the foundation and, alongside both private and community support, will cycle back into the community through our giving programs. Currently, those include the FreshGrass Awards, the FreshGrass Commission, FreshScores, FreshGrass Presents, and the *No Depression* Writing Fellowship (see freshgrass.org for details).

We feel that establishing ourselves as a nonprofit gives us a stable platform to be a voice and catalyst for the roots music industry. It is our great hope that artists, fans, labels, and other businesses in our corner of the world will support our efforts, knowing that our success will be a shared success.

Pulling all of this together is a small staff of six people scattered all over the country – Raleigh, Asheville, San Francisco, Austin, and Seattle. But equally critical to our efforts is more than 25 staff writers, columnists, correspondents, accountants, and interns keeping the ND website humming and fresh. To boot, the team from MASS MoCA manages and runs the festival each year, while the Office of the Performing Arts in New York City manages the grant programs and event bookings, among many other things.

In addition, we have multiple partners, sponsors, advertisers, and donors who help keep the lights on, plus an ever-longer list of musicians who have shared their stories, time, and energy to support us. And, of course, there are the 150,000+ of you who have participated along the way by contributing, reading, commenting, visiting, purchasing, and otherwise making all of this work. In short, we have the equivalent of a small town trying to push this mission ahead, and we could not be more excited about where this will lead.